Advanced Analytics with R and Tableau

Advanced analytics using data classification, unsupervised learning and data visualization

Jen Stirrup

Ruben Oliva Ramos

BIRMINGHAM - MUMBAI

Advanced Analytics with R and Tableau

First published: August 2017

Production reference: 1180817

Published by Packt Publishing Ltd.
Livery Place
35 Livery Street
Birmingham B3 2PB, UK.

ISBN 978-1-78646-011-0

www.packtpub.com

Credits

Authors
Jen Stirrup
Ruben Oliva Ramos

Reviewers
Kyle Johnson
Radovan Kavicky
Juan Tomás Oliva Ramos
Lourdes Bolaños Pérez

Commissioning Editor
Veena Pagare

Acquisition Editor
Vinay Argekar

Content Development Editor
Aishwarya Pandere

Technical Editor
Karan Thakkar

Copy Editor
Safis Editing

Project Coordinator
Nidhi Joshi

Proofreader
Safis Editing

Indexer
Tejal Daruwale Soni

Graphics
Tania Dutta

Production Coordinator
Arvindkumar Gupta

Cover Work
Arvindkumar Gupta

About the Authors

Jen Stirrup, recently named as one of the top 9 most influential business intelligence female experts in the world by Solutions Review, is a Microsoft Data. Platform MVP, and PASS Director-At-Large, is a well-known business intelligence and data visualization expert, author, data strategist, and community advocate who has been peer-recognized as one of the top 100 most global influential tweeters on big data and analytics topics.

Specialties: business intelligence, Microsoft SQL Server, Tableau, architecture, data, R, Hadoop, and Hive. Jen is passionate about all things data and business intelligence, helping leaders derive value from data. For two decades, Jen has worked in artificial intelligence and business intelligence consultancy, architecting, and delivering and supporting complex enterprise solutions for customers all over the world.

I would like to thank the reviewers of this book for their valuable comments and suggestions. I would also like to thank the wonderful team at Packt for publishing the book and helping me all along.

I'd like to thank my son Matthew for his unending patience, and my Coton de Tuléar puppy Archie for his long walks. I'd also like to thank my parents, Margaret and Drew, for their incredible support for this globe-trotting single mother who isn't always the best daughter that they deserve. They are the parents that I want to be.

I'd like to thank the Microsoft teams for their patience and support; they deserve special recognition here. I am grateful for their love and support, and for generally humouring me when I go off and do another community venture focused on my passions for their technology and diversity in the tech community.

I'd like to thank Tableau: Bora Beran who kindly got in touch, Andy Cotgreave who keeps the Tableau community fun and engaging as well as educational, and the Tableau UK team for humouring me, too. I am seeing a pattern here.

Ruben Oliva Ramos is a computer systems engineer from Tecnologico of León Institute with a master's degree in computer and electronic systems engineering, tele informatics, and networking specialization from University of Salle Bajio in Leon, Guanajuato, Mexico. He has more than five years' experience in developing web applications to control and monitor devices connected with the Arduino and Raspberry Pi using web frameworks and cloud services to build Internet of Things applications.

He is a mechatronics teacher at University of Salle Bajio and teaches students studying for their master's degree in Design and Engineering of Mechatronics Systems. He also works at Centro de Bachillerato Tecnologico Industrial 225 in Leon, Guanajuato, Mexico, teaching electronics, robotics and control, automation, and microcontrollers at Mechatronics Technician Career.

He has worked on consultant and developer projects in areas such as monitoring systems and datalogger data using technologies such as Android, iOS, Windows Phone, Visual Studio .NET, HTML5, PHP, CSS, Ajax, JavaScript, Angular, ASP .NET databases (SQLite, MongoDB, and MySQL), and web servers (Node.js and IIS). Ruben has done hardware programming on the Arduino, Raspberry Pi, Ethernet Shield, GPS, and GSM/GPRS, ESP8266, control and monitor systems for data acquisition and programming.

He's the Author at Pack Publishing book: Internet of Things Programming with JavaScript.

About the Reviewers

Kyle Johnson is a data scientist based out of Pittsburgh Pennsylvania. He has a Masters Degree in Information Systems Management from Carnegie Mellon University and a Bachelors Degree in Psychology from Grove City College. He is an adjunct data science professor at Carnegie Mellon, and his applied work focuses in the healthcare and life sciences domain. See his LinkedIn page for an updated resume and contact information: https://www.linkedin.com/in/kljohnson721.

I would like to thank Nancy, George and Helena.

Radovan Kavický is the principal data scientist and president at GapData Institute based in Bratislava, Slovakia, where he harnesses the power of data & wisdom of economics for public good. With an academic background in macroeconomics, he is a consultant and analyst by profession, with more than eight years of experience in consulting for clients from public and private sectors along with strong mathematical and analytical skills and the ability to deliver top-level research and analytical work.

He switched to Python, R, and Tableau from MATLAB, SAS, and Stata. Besides being a member of the Slovak Economic Association (SEA), Evangelist of Open Data, Open Budget Initiative, & Open Government Partnership, he is also the founder of PyData Bratislava, R <- Slovakia, and SK/CZ Tableau User Group (skczTUG). He has been the speaker at TechSummit (Bratislava, 2017) and at PyData (Berlin, 2017). He is also a member of the global Tableau #DataLeader network (2017).

You can follow him on Twitter at @radovankavicky, @GapDataInst, or @PyDataBA

For his full profile and experience, visit https://www.linkedin.com/in/radovankavicky/, https://github.com/radovankavicky, and GapData Institute, https://www.gapdata.org.

Juan Tomás Oliva Ramos is an environmental engineer from the university of Guanajuato, with a master's degree in Administrative engineering and quality. He has more than five years of experience in: Management and development of patents, technological innovation projects and Development of technological solutions through the statistical control of processes.

He is a teacher of Statistics, Entrepreneurship and Technological development of projects since 2011. He has always maintained an interest for the improvement and the innovation in the processes through the technology. He became an entrepreneur mentor, technology management consultant and started a new department of technology management and entrepreneurship at Instituto Tecnologico Superior de Purisima del Rincon.

He has worked in the book: Wearable designs for Smart watches, Smart TV's and Android mobile devices

He has developed prototypes through programming and automation technologies for the improvement of operations, which have been registered to apply for his patent.

I want to thank God God for giving me wisdom and humility to review this book. I want thank Rubén, for inviting me to collaborate on this adventure. I want to thank my wife, Brenda, our two magic princesses (Regina and Renata) and our next member (Tadeo), All of you are my strengths, happiness and my desire to look for the best for you.

www.PacktPub.com

eBooks, discount offers, and more

Did you know that Packt offers eBook versions of every book published, with PDF and ePub files available? You can upgrade to the eBook version at `www.PacktPub.com` and as a print book customer, you are entitled to a discount on the eBook copy. Get in touch with us at `customercare@packtpub.com` for more details.

At `www.PacktPub.com`, you can also read a collection of free technical articles, sign up for a range of free newsletters and receive exclusive discounts and offers on Packt books and eBooks.

`https://www.packtpub.com/mapt`

Get the most in-demand software skills with Mapt. Mapt gives you full access to all Packt books and video courses, as well as industry-leading tools to help you plan your personal development and advance your career.

Why subscribe?

- Fully searchable across every book published by Packt
- Copy and paste, print, and bookmark content
- On demand and accessible via a web browser

Customer Feedback

Thanks for purchasing this Packt book. At Packt, quality is at the heart of our editorial process. To help us improve, please leave us an honest review on this book's Amazon page at `https://www.amazon.com/dp/1786460114`.

If you'd like to join our team of regular reviewers, you can e-mail us at `customerreviews@packtpub.com`. We award our regular reviewers with free eBooks and videos in exchange for their valuable feedback. Help us be relentless in improving our products!

Table of Contents

Preface

Moving from data visualization into deeper, more advanced analytics, this book will intensify data skills for data-savvy users who want to move into analytics and data science in order to enhance their businesses by harnessing the analytical power of R and the stunning visualization capabilities of Tableau.

Together, Tableau and R offer accessible analytics by allowing a combination of easy-to-use data visualization along with industry-standard, robust statistical computation. Readers will come across a wide range of machine learning algorithms and learn how descriptive, prescriptive, predictive, and visually appealing analytical solutions can be designed with R and Tableau.

In order to maximize learning, hands-on examples will ease the transition from being a data-savvy user to a data analyst using sound statistical tools to perform advanced analytics.

Tableau (uniquely) offers excellent visualization combined with advanced analytics; R is at the pinnacle of statistical computational languages. When you want to move from one view of data to another, backed up by complex computations, the combination of R and Tableau is the perfect solution. This example-rich guide will teach you how to combine these two to perform advanced analytics by integrating Tableau with R to create beautiful data visualizations.

What this book covers

Chapter 1, Getting Ready for Tableau and R, shows how to connect Tableau Desktop with R through calculated fields and take advantage of R functions, libraries, packages, and even saved models. We'll also cover Tableau Server configuration with R through an instance of Rserve (through the tabadmin utility), allowing anyone to view a dashboard containing R functionality. Combining R with Tableau gives you the ability to bring deep statistical analysis into a drag-and-drop visual analytics environment.

Chapter 2, The Power of R, integrates both the platforms in the previous chapter; we'll walk through different ways in which readers can use R to combine and compare data for analysis. We will cover, with examples, the core essentials of R programming such as variables, data structures in R, control mechanisms in R, and how to execute these commands in R before proceeding to later chapters that heavily rely on these concepts to script complex analytical operations.

Chapter 3, A Methodology for Advanced Analytics using Tableau and R, creates a roadmap for our analytics investigation. You'll learn how to assess the performance of both supervised and unsupervised learning algorithms, and the importance of testing. Using R and Tableau, we will explore why and how you should split your data into a training set and a test set. In order to understand how to display the data accurately as well as beautifully in Tableau, the concepts of bias and variance are explained.

Chapter 4, Prediction with R and Tableau Using Regression, considers regression from an analytics point of view. In this chapter, we look at the predictive capabilities and performance of regression algorithms. At the end of this chapter, you'll have experience in simple linear regression, multi-linear regression, and k-nearest neighbors regression using a business-oriented understanding of the actual use cases of regression techniques.

Chapter 5, Classifying Data with Tableau, shows ways to perform classification using R and visualize the results in Tableau. Classification is one of the most important tasks in analytics today. By the end of this chapter, you'll build a decision tree and classify unseen observations with k-nearest neighbors, with a focus on a business-oriented understanding of the business question using classification algorithms.

Chapter 6, Advanced Analytics Using Clustering, gives a business-oriented understanding of the business questions using clustering algorithms and applying visualization techniques that best suit the scenario.

Chapter 7, Advanced Analytics with Unsupervised Learning, teaches k-means clustering and hierarchical clustering. It has a business-oriented understanding of the business question using unsupervised learning algorithms.

Chapter 8, Interpreting Your Results for Your Audience. How do you interpret the results and the numbers when you have them? What does a p-value mean? Analytical investigations will result in a variety of relationships in data, but the audience may have problems understanding the results. Statistical tests state a null and an alternative hypothesis, and then calculate a test statistic and report an associated p-value. In this chapter, we will look at ways in which we can answer "what if?" questions and applicable customer scenarios using cohort analysis, with a focus on how we can display the results so that the audience can make a conclusion from the tests.

What you need for this book

You'll need the following software:

- R version 3.4.1
- RStudio for Windows
- Plugins for RStudio

Who this book is for

This book will appeal to Tableau users who want to go beyond the Tableau interface and deploy the full potential of Tableau, by using R to perform advanced analytics with Tableau.

A basic familiarity with R is useful but not compulsory, as the book starts off with concrete examples of R and will move on quickly to more advanced spheres of analytics using online data sources to support hands-on learning. Those R developers who want to integrate R with Tableau will also benefit from this book.

Conventions

In this book, you will find a number of text styles that distinguish between different kinds of information. Here are some examples of these styles and an explanation of their meaning.

Code words in text, database table names, folder names, filenames, file extensions, pathnames, dummy URLs, user input, and Twitter handles are shown as follows: "We can include other contexts through the use of the include directive."

A block of code is set as follows:

```
df = data.frame(
Year=c(2013, 2013, 2013),
Country=c("Arab World","Carribean States", "Central Europe"),
LifeExpectancy=c(71, 72, 76))
```

Any command-line input or output is written as follows:

```
IrisBySpecies <- split(iris,iris$Species)
```

New terms and **important words** are shown in bold. Words that you see on the screen, for example, in menus or dialog boxes, appear in the text like this:"You can now just click on Stream to access the live stream from the camera."

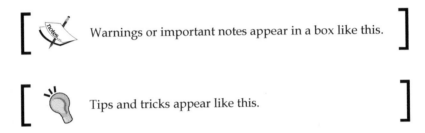

Warnings or important notes appear in a box like this.

Tips and tricks appear like this.

Reader feedback

Feedback from our readers is always welcome. Let us know what you think about this book—what you liked or disliked. Reader feedback is important for us as it helps us develop titles that you will really get the most out of.

To send us general feedback, simply e-mail feedback@packtpub.com, and mention the book's title in the subject of your message.

If there is a topic that you have expertise in and you are interested in either writing or contributing to a book, see our author guide at www.packtpub.com/authors.

Customer support

Now that you are the proud owner of a Packt book, we have a number of things to help you to get the most from your purchase.

Downloading the example code

You can download the example code files for this book from your account at
`http://www.packtpub.com`. If you purchased this book elsewhere, you can visit
`http://www.packtpub.com/support` and register to have the files e-mailed directly
to you.

You can download the code files by following these steps:

1. Log in or register to our website using your e-mail address and password.
2. Hover the mouse pointer on the **SUPPORT** tab at the top.
3. Click on **Code Downloads & Errata**.
4. Enter the name of the book in the **Search** box.
5. Select the book for which you're looking to download the code files.
6. Choose from the drop-down menu where you purchased this book from.
7. Click on **Code Download**.

You can also download the code files by clicking on the **Code Files** button on the
book's webpage at the Packt Publishing website. This page can be accessed by
entering the book's name in the **Search** box. Please note that you need to be logged in
to your Packt account.

Once the file is downloaded, please make sure that you unzip or extract the folder
using the latest version of:

* WinRAR / 7-Zip for Windows
* Zipeg / iZip / UnRarX for Mac
* 7-Zip / PeaZip for Linux

The code bundle for the book is also hosted on GitHub at `https://github.com/
PacktPublishing/Advanced-Analytics-with-R-and-Tableau`. We also have
other code bundles from our rich catalog of books and videos available at `https://
github.com/PacktPublishing/`. Check them out!

Errata

Although we have taken every care to ensure the accuracy of our content, mistakes do happen. If you find a mistake in one of our books—maybe a mistake in the text or the code—we would be grateful if you could report this to us. By doing so, you can save other readers from frustration and help us improve subsequent versions of this book. If you find any errata, please report them by visiting http://www.packtpub.com/submit-errata, selecting your book, clicking on the **Errata Submission Form** link, and entering the details of your errata. Once your errata are verified, your submission will be accepted and the errata will be uploaded to our website or added to any list of existing errata under the Errata section of that title.

To view the previously submitted errata, go to https://www.packtpub.com/books/content/support and enter the name of the book in the search field. The required information will appear under the **Errata** section.

Piracy

Piracy of copyrighted material on the Internet is an ongoing problem across all media. At Packt, we take the protection of our copyright and licenses very seriously. If you come across any illegal copies of our works in any form on the Internet, please provide us with the location address or website name immediately so that we can pursue a remedy.

Please contact us at copyright@packtpub.com with a link to the suspected pirated material.

We appreciate your help in protecting our authors and our ability to bring you valuable content.

Questions

If you have a problem with any aspect of this book, you can contact us at questions@packtpub.com, and we will do our best to address the problem.

1
Advanced Analytics with R and Tableau

Moving from data visualization into deeper, more advanced analytics? This book will intensify data skills for a data-savvy user who wants to move into analytics and data science in order to make a difference to their businesses, by harnessing the analytical power of R and the stunning visualization capabilities of Tableau.

Together, Tableau and R offer accessible analytics by allowing a combination of easy-to-use data visualization along with industry-standard, robust statistical computation. Readers will come across a wide range of machine learning algorithms and learn how descriptive, prescriptive, and predictive visually appealing analytical solutions can be designed solutions with R and Tableau.

Let's get ready to start our transition from being a data-savvy user to a data analyst using sound statistical tools to perform advanced analytics. To do this, we need to get the tools ready. In this topic, we will commence our journey of conducting Tableau analytics with the industry-standard, statistical prowess of R. As the first step on our journey, we will cover the installation of R, including key points about ensuring the right bitness before we start. In order to create R scripts easily, we will install RStudio for ease of use.

We need to get R and Tableau to communicate, and to achieve this communication, we will install and configure **Rserve**.

Installing R for Windows

The following steps shows how to download and install R on windows:

1. The first step is to download your required version of R from the CRAN website [http://www.rproject.org/].

2. Go to the official R website, which you can find at https://www.r-project.org/.

3. The download link can be found on the left-hand side of the page.

4. The next option is for you to choose the location of the server that holds R. The best option is to choose the mirror that is geographically closest to you. For example, if you are based in the UK, then you might choose the mirror that is located in Bristol.

5. Once you click on the link, there is a section at the top of the page called **Download and Install R**. There is a different link for each operating system. To download the Windows-specific version of R, there is a link that specifies Download R for Windows. When you click on it, the download links will appear on the next page to download R.

6. On the next page, there are a number of options, but it is easier to select the option that specifies install R for the first time.

7. Finally, there is an option at the top of the page that allows you to download the latest R installation package. The install package is wrapped up in an EXE file, and both 32 bit and 64 bit options are wrapped up in the same file.

    Now that R is downloaded, the next step is to install R. The instructions are given here:

8. Double-click on the R executable file, and select the language. In this example, we will use **English**. Choose your preferred language, and click **OK** to proceed:

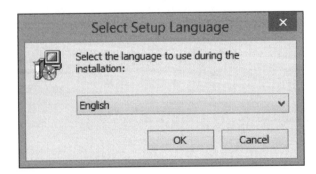

9. The Welcome page will appear, and you should click **Next** to continue:

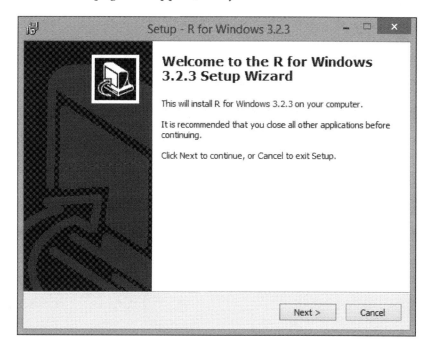

10. The next item is the general license agreement. Click **Next** to continue:

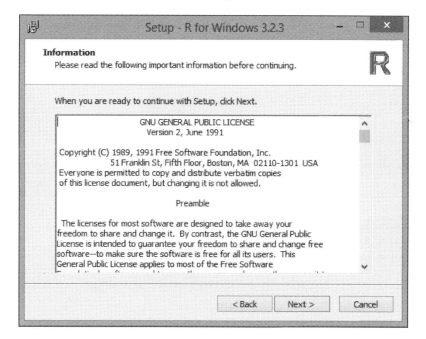

11. The next step is to specify the destination location for R's files. In this example, the default is selected. Once the destination has been selected, click **Next** to proceed:

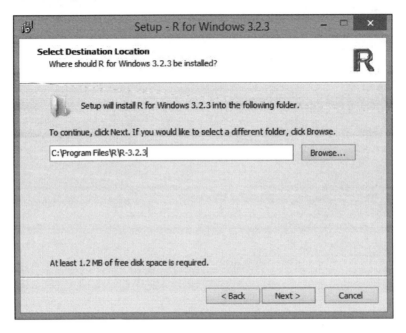

12. In the next step, the components of R are configured. If you have a 32-bit machine, then you will need to select the 32-bit option from the drop-down list.

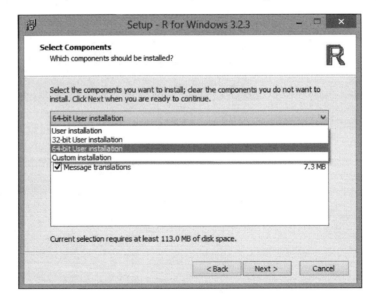

13. In the next screenshot, the **64-bit User Installation** option has been selected:

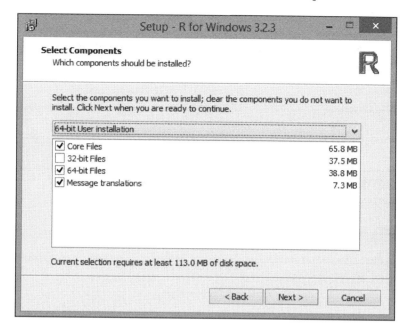

14. The next option is to customize the startup options. Here, the default is selected. Click **Next** to continue.

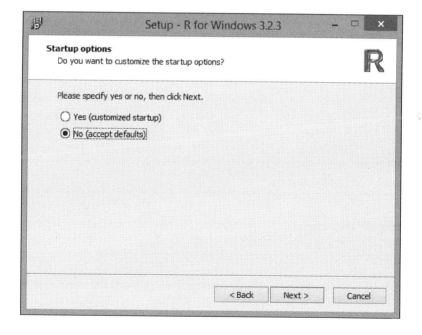

15. The next option is to select the **Start Menu folder** configuration. Select the default, and click **Next**:

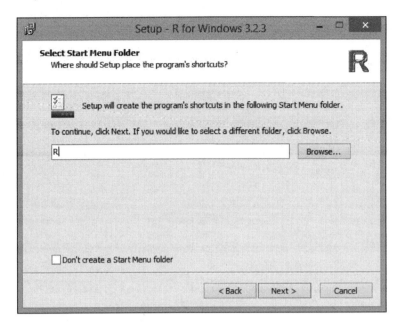

16. Next, it's possible to configure some of R's options, such as the creation of a desktop icon. Here, let's choose the default options and click **Next**:

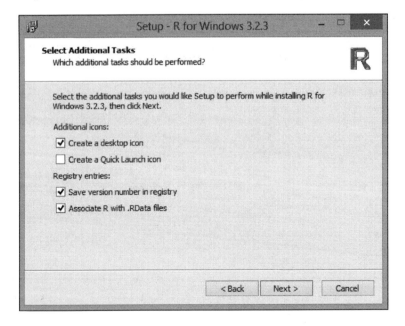

17. In the next step, the R files are copied to the computer. This step should only take a few moments:

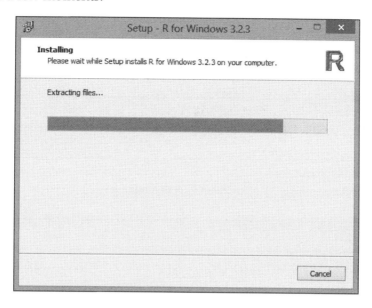

18. Finally, R is installed, and you should receive a final window. Click **Finish**:

19. Once completed, launch **RGui** from the shortcut, or you can locate RGui.exe from your installation path. The default path for Windows is C:\Program Files\R\R- 2.15.1\bin\x64\Rgui.exe.

20. Type `help.start()` at the R-Console prompt and press *Enter*. If you can see the help server page then you have successfully installed and configured your R package.

RStudio

The R interface is not particularly intuitive for beginners. For this reason, RStudio IDE, the desktop version, is an excellent option for interacting with R. The download and installation sequence is provided.

There are two versions; the RStudio Desktop version, and the paid RStudio Server version. In this book, we will focus on the RStudio Desktop IDE option, which is open source.

Prerequisites for RStudio installation

In this section, RStudio IDE is installed on the Windows 10 operating system:

1. To download RStudio, you can retrieve it from `https://www.rstudio.com/products/rstudio-desktop/`.

2. Once you have downloaded RStudio, double-click on the file to start the installation. This will display the RStudio Setup and Welcome page. Click **Next** to continue:

3. The next option allows the user to configure the installation location for RStudio. Here, the default option has been retained. If you do change the location, you can click **Browse** to select your preferred installation folder. Once you've selected your folder, click **Next** to continue to the next step.

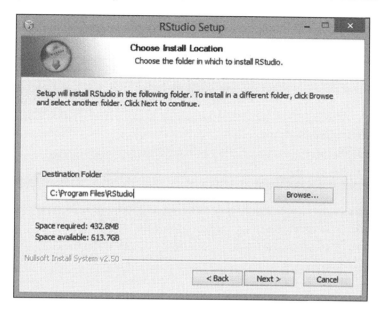

4. In the next step, RStudio shortcuts are specified. Click on **Install** to proceed:

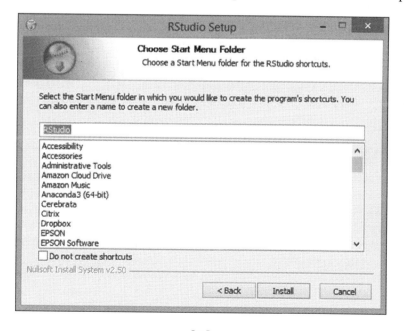

5. RStudio installs in the next step:

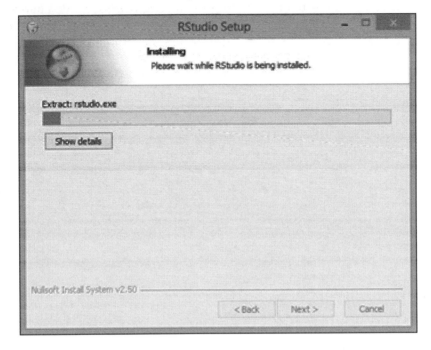

6. Once completed, launch RStudio IDE. You can find it by navigating to **Start | All Programs | RStudio | RStudio.exe**. Alternatively, you can type RStudio into the Cortana search box. If you specified a custom installation directory, then you can find RStudio as an EXE file. The default installation directory for RStudio IDE is `C:\Program Files\RStudio\bin\rstudio.exe`.

7. Type `help.start()` at the RStudio prompt and press *Enter*. If you can see the help files on the screen then you have successfully installed and configured RStudio IDE to run with R.

Implementing the scripts for the book

Now that we have installed R and RStudio, we can download and install the scripts for this book. This book's scripts and code can be found on GitHub. If the reader hasn't got a free GitHub account, then it's recommended that Git and GitHub are set up. It's good practice for storing your own R scripts at a later date. If required, the reader is referred to the GitHub site for more details. GitHub itself can be found at `github.com`. Training material can be found at `https://training.github.com/kit/`.

After setting up Git and GitHub, you can download our data and scripts by taking a copy of this book's GitHub repository. Simply put, a fork is a copy of a repository, and it means that you can freely experiment with changes without affecting the original project. Please refer to the GitHub training material for more information on how to fork a repository, download data and scripts, and how to keep your local copy in sync with changes to the repository.

> Go to the GitHub repo at `https://github.com/datarelish/Advanced-AnalyticsRandTableauBook`.

At the top right-hand corner of the page, click **Fork**. This means you have forked the repository. The next step is to download the files to your local computer. To do this, you can run the following line of code in your Git Bash:

```
git clone https://github.com/datarelish/Advanced-
AnalyticsRandTableauBook
```

Testing the scripting

Before we proceed, let's proceed to run a script to test that our setup works:

1. Open the script in RStudio's script editor.
2. Go to the **Code** menu item.
3. Choose **Source** from the menu.
4. Navigate to the `Packt Tableau and R Book Setup.r` file.
5. Press *Ctrl + A* to select the whole script.
6. In the script window, click **Run**.
7. You should see the results in the output window.

Tableau and R connectivity using Rserve

Rserve is a server that allows applications to access R functionality. It allows you to use a series of functions to pass R expressions to an Rserve server and obtain a result.

If you upload a workbook that contains R functionality to the Tableau server, then the Tableau server must have a connection to an Rserve server. See R Connection, in the Tableau Desktop help, for details.

R is not supported for Tableau Reader or Tableau Online.

In this section, we will install, run, and configure Rserve.

Installing Rserve

To install and run Rserve, follow these steps:

1. Open RStudio and go to the **Install Packages** tab on the interface.

2. In the **Packages** textbox, type `Rserve` and click **OK**.

3. Rserve will install, and you will see the output messages in the RStudio Console. When it is finished, you will see the chevron again.

4. Now, open **Control Panel** on the server, and search for **environment variable** in the search box.

5. Click on the **Edit the System Environment Variables** option.

6. Add a new variable to the PATH variable path. Add the directory containing `R.dll` to your path environment variable. For example, `C:\Program Files\R\R-3.0.2\bin\x64`.

7. You should see the new path in the **Edit Environment Variable** window. You can see a sample image here:

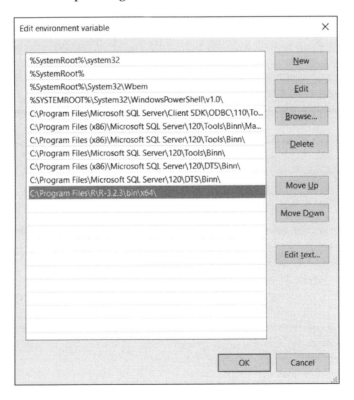

8. Click **OK**.

Let's check that Rserve is running properly:

In RStudio, let's call Rserve by running the following command in the RStudio Console:

```
library(Rserve)
```

Configuring an Rserve Connection

To configure an Rserve connection, follow these steps:

1. On the **Help** menu in Tableau Desktop, choose **Settings** and **Performance | Manage R Connection** to open the Rserve connection dialog box.
2. Enter or select a server name using a domain name or an IP address.
3. Specify a port (Port 6311) is the default port for Rserve servers.
4. If the server requires credentials, specify a username and password.
5. Click **Test Connection**.
6. Click **OK**.

Summary

In this chapter, we started on our journey of conducting Tableau analytics with the industry-standard, statistical prowess of R. In this chapter, we covered the installation of R, including a key point about ensuring the right bitness before we start. We also installed RStudio and ran a script, as a way of engaging with R. Finally, we installed and configured Rserve for Tableau.

In our next chapter, we will learn more about the underlying data structures of R so that we can make use of the analytic power of Tableau and R more effectively.

2
The Power of R

Having understood how to integrate both the platforms in the previous chapter, we'll walk through the different ways in which you can use R to combine and compare data for analysis.

We will cover, with examples, the core essentials of R programming such as variables and data structures in R such as matrices, factors, vectors, and data frames. We will also focus on control mechanisms in R (relational operators, logical operators, conditional statements, loops, functions, and apply) and how to execute these commands in R to get grips with it before proceeding to chapters that heavily rely on these concepts for scripting complex analytical operations.

Core essentials of R programming

One of the reasons for R's success is its use of variables. Variables are used in all aspects of R programming. For example, variables can hold data, strings to access a database, whole models, queries, and test results. Variables are a key part of the modeling process, and their selection has a fundamental impact on the usefulness of the models. Therefore, variables are an important place to start since they are at the heart of R programming.

Variables

In the following section we will deal with the variables—how to create variables and working with variables.

Creating variables

It is very simple to create variables in R, and to save values in them. To create a variable, you simply need to give the variable a name, and assign a value to it.

In many other languages, such as SQL, it's necessary to specify the type of value that the variable will hold. So, for example, if the variable is designed to hold an integer or a string, then this is specified at the point at which the variable is created.

Unlike other programming languages, such as SQL, R does not require that you specify the type of the variable before it is created. Instead, R works out the type for itself, by looking at the data that is assigned to the variable.

In R, we assign variables using an assignment variable, which is a less than sign (<) followed by a hyphen (-). Put together, the assignment variable looks like so:

Working with variables

It is important to understand what is contained in the variables. It is easy to check the content of the variables using the `ls` command. If you need more details of the variables, then the `ls.str` command will provide you with more information.

If you need to remove variables, then you can use the `rm` function.

Data structures in R

The power of R resides in its ability to analyze data, and this ability is largely derived from its powerful data types. Fundamentally, R is a vectorized programming language. Data structures in R are constructed from vectors that are foundational. This means that R's operations are optimized to work with vectors.

Vector

The vector is a core component of R. It is a fundamental data type. Essentially, a vector is a data structure that contains an array where all of the values are the same type. For example, they could all be strings, or numbers. However, note that vectors cannot contain mixed data types.

R uses the `c()` function to take a list of items and turns them into a vector.

Lists

R contains two types of lists: a basic list, and a named list. A basic list is created using the `list()` operator. In a named list, every item in the list has a name as well as a value. named lists are a good mapping structure to help map data between R and Tableau. In R, lists are mapped using the `$` operator. Note, however, that the list label operators are case sensitive.

Matrices

Matrices are two-dimensional structures that have rows and columns. The matrices are lists of rows. It's important to note that every cell in a matrix has the same type.

Factors

A factor is a list of all possible values of a variable in a string format. It is a special string type, which is chosen from a specified set of values known as levels. They are sometimes known as categorical variables. In dimensional modeling terminology, a factor is equivalent to a dimension, and the levels represent different attributes of the dimension. Note that factors are variables that can only contain a limited number of different values.

Data frames

The data frame is the main data structure in R. It's possible to envisage the data frame as a table of data, with rows and columns. Unlike the list structure, the data frame can contain different types of data. In R, we use the `data.frame()` command in order to create a data frame.

The data frame is extremely flexible for working with structured data, and it can ingest data from many different data types. Two main ways to ingest data into data frames involves the use of many data connectors, which connect to data sources such as databases, for example. There is also a command, `read.table()`, which takes in data.

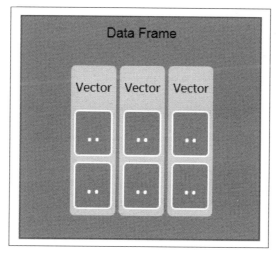

Data Frame Structure

Here is an example, populated data frame. There are three columns, and two rows. The top of the data frame is the header. Each row holds a line of data row, starting with the row name, and then followed by the data itself. Each data member of a row is called a cell.

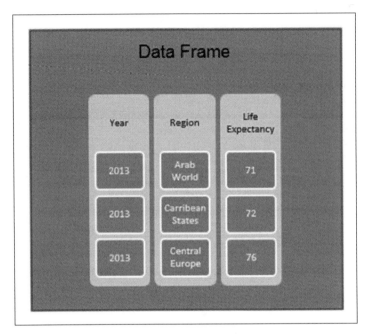

Example Data Frame Structure

In R, we can create data frames by accessing external data, or we can create our own data frames by assigning data to a variable. Let's set up our own example data frame, populated with data:

```
df = data.frame(
Year=c(2013, 2013, 2013),
Country=c("Arab World","Carribean States", "Central Europe"),
LifeExpectancy=c(71, 72, 76))
```

As always, we should read out at least some of the data frame so we can double-check that it was set correctly. The data frame was set to the `df` variable, so we can read out the contents by simply typing in the variable name at the command prompt:

```
Console ~/Packt/
> df
  Year         Country LifeExpectancy
1 2013       Arab World             71
2 2013 Caribbean States             72
3 2013    Central Europe            76
```

Variable printout to the R Console

To obtain the data held in a cell, we enter the row and column co-ordinates of the cell, and surround them by square brackets ([]). In this example, if we wanted to obtain the value of the second cell in the second row, then we would use the following:

```
df[2, "Country"]
```

We can also conduct summary statistics on our data frame. For example, if we use the following command:

```
summary(df)
```

Then we obtain the summary statistics of the data. The example output is as follows:

```
Console ~/Packt/
> summary(df)
      Year              Country   LifeExpectancy
 Min.   :2013   Arab World      :1   Min.   :71.0
 1st Qu.:2013   Caribbean States:1   1st Qu.:71.5
 Median :2013   Central Europe  :1   Median :72.0
 Mean   :2013                        Mean   :73.0
 3rd Qu.:2013                        3rd Qu.:74.0
 Max.   :2013                        Max.   :76.0
```

Summary Statistics printout to the R Console

You'll notice that the summary command has summarized different values for each of the columns. It has identified `Year` as an integer, and produced the `Min`, Quartiles, `Mean`, and `Max` for the year. The `Country` column has been listed, simply because it does not contain any numeric values. `Life Expectancy` is summarized correctly.

We can change the `Year` column to a factor, using the following command:

```
df$Year <- as.factor(df$Year)
```

Then, we can rerun the summary command again:

```
summary(df)
```

On this occasion, the data frame now returns the correct results that we expect:

```
> summary(df)
     Year                Country    LifeExpectancy
  2013:3    Arab World       :1    Min.    :71.0
            Carribean States:1    1st Qu. :71.5
            Central Europe   :1    Median  :72.0
                                   Mean    :73.0
                                   3rd Qu. :74.0
                                   Max.    :76.0
```

Variable printout to the R Console

As we proceed throughout this book, we will be building on more useful features that will help us to analyze data using data structures, and visualize the data in interesting ways using R.

When we consume data from online data sources, it's worth double-checking the data types in the source data. The summary(df) command is very useful.

We can retrieve data in Tableau, using commands that we have used so far in this Chapter. Firstly, however, we need to make sure that Rserve is installed and running. Let's check the installation first, with the command:

```
install.packages("Rserve")
```

Once the command has executed, we need to call the package so we can use it throughout the script:

```
library(Rserve)
```

Next, we can start the **Rserve** service with the following command:

```
Rserve()
```

In this example, however, we are simply going to work with the CSV file that contains the data. To do this, let's open up a new Tableau workbook, and we will choose excel as our format.

Now, let's connect live to the excel data source. When we connect to the data in Tableau, we can see the interface here:

As a piece of terminology, note that R talks about variables. In tableau, we talk about dimensions and when we use the Dimension **Year as String**, plus the **Value**, we get horizontal bars.

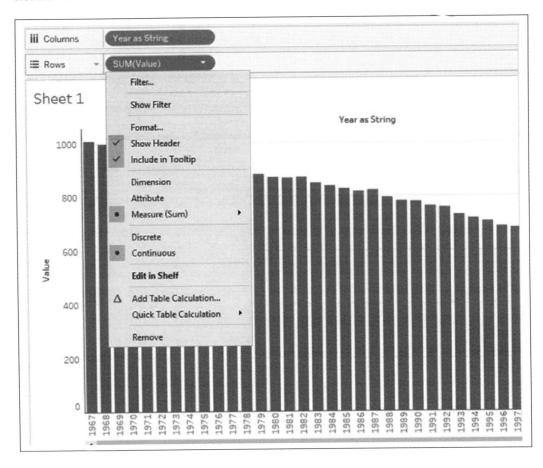

We can start to add in the country, which appears as follows:

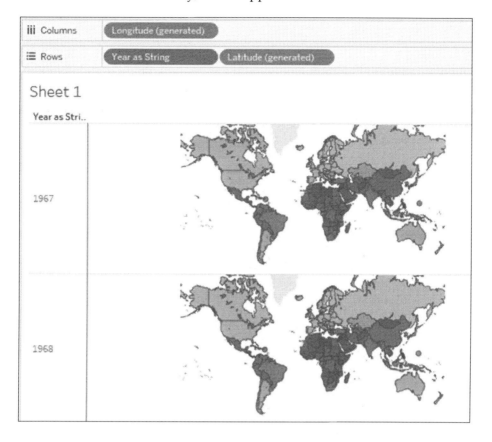

However, this doesn't really give a sense of the changes over time, which is our preferred end result. To achieve this objective, let's look at the box-and-whisker plot.

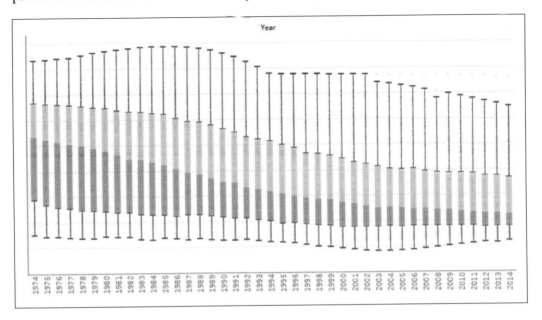

Here, it's clearer to see that the fertility rate has been descending over time. Let's focus on just a few countries – Rwanda, Norway, and the United States

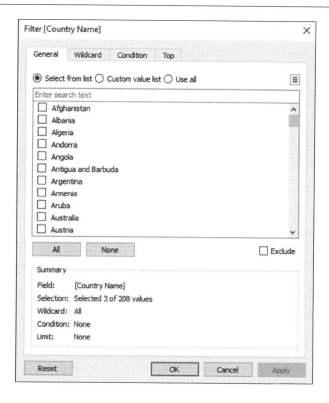

We can filter our selection down to the countries that we are most interested in.
Now, we can see patterns in the data more clearly.

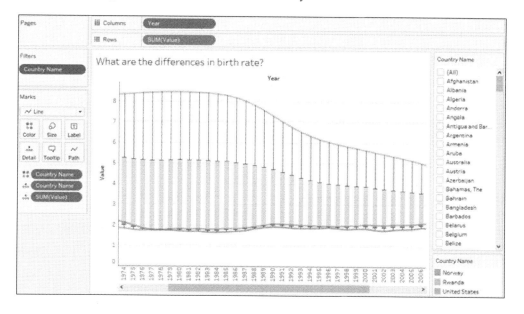

A few simple changes have helped to illuminate the data:

We can see that the USA and Norway track one another very closely. Rwanda, on the other hand, has the highest birth rate, which falls down over the years. The tops of the box-and-whisker plots have been changed to show a line, in order to emphasise how this metric has changed over time.

What do the box-and-whisker plot lines actually mean? They tell us something individually about the range between the minimum and maximum numbers. Here is an example diagram:

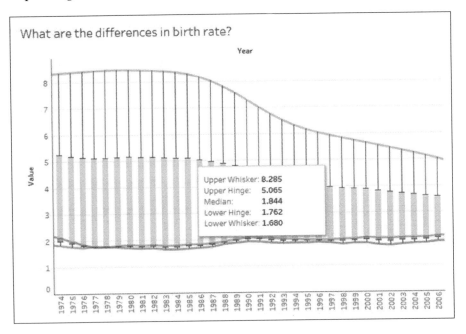

Rwanda is the upper whisker – meaning the maximum. The first and third quartiles are given, along with the median.

The tooltip gives the viewer additional details. It is provided 'on demand', when the user hovers over that part of the chart.

To summarise, we have seen how R and Tableau can be used together in order to display data better. Generally speaking, it is better to change the data closer to the source rather than leaving it until the front end. The reason for this is that you have only changed the data once, which then propagates through to other data sources and worksheets. It's not required for you to change it every time.

Now that we have seen a simple example of how R and Tableau can work together, let's look at more complex R programming constructs.

Control structures in R

R has the appearance of a procedural programming language. However, it is built on another language, known as **S** programming language. S leans towards functional programming. It also has some object-oriented characteristics. This means that there are many complexities in the way that R works.

In this section, we will look at some of the fundamental building blocks that make up key control structures in R, and then we will move onto looping and vectorized operations.

Assignment operators

R has five assignment operators, which are listed here:

```
<-
```

```
->
```

```
=
```

```
<<-
```

```
->>
```

In this book, we will use the following assignment operator:

```
<-
```

We will use this assignment operator here, because it is used commonly in examples on well-known internet sites such as **StackOverflow** (http://stackoverflow. com/). It's also possible to use the rightward assignment operator, but that is confusing for many people so it is not used here. Note also that the equals sign isn't used here, because it is often used to mean equality. Therefore, it's clearer to use the leftward assignment operator.

Logical operators

Logical operators are binary operators that allow the comparison of values:

Operator	Description
<	less than
<=	less than or equal to
>	greater than

Operator	Description
>=	greater than or equal to
==	exactly equal to
!=	not equal to
!x	Not x
x | y	x OR y
x & y	x AND y
isTRUE(x)	test if X is TRUE

For loops and vectorization in R

Specifically, we will look at the constructs involved in loops. Note, however, that it is more efficient to use vectorized operations rather than loops, because R is vector-based. We investigate loops here, because they are a good first step in understanding how R works, and then we can optimize this understanding by focusing on vectorized alternatives that are more efficient.

More information about control flows can be obtained by executing the command at the command line:

```
Help?Control
```

The control flow commands take decisions and make decisions between alternative actions. The main constructs are for, while, and repeat.

For loops

Let's look at a for loop in more detail. For this exercise, we will use the Fisher iris dataset, which is installed along with R by default. We are going to produce summary statistics for each species of iris in the dataset.

You can see some of the iris data by typing in the following command at the command prompt:

```
head(iris)
```

We can divide the iris dataset so that the data is split by species. To do this, we use the split command, and we assign it to the variable called IrisBySpecies:

```
IrisBySpecies <- split(iris,iris$Species)
```

Now, we can use a `for` loop in order to process the data in order to summarize it by species.

Firstly, we will set up a variable called output, and set it to a list type. For each species held in the `IrisBySpecies` variable, we set it to calculate the minimum, maximum, mean, and total cases. It is then set to a data frame called `output.df`, which is printed out to the screen:

```
output <- list()
for(n in names(IrisBySpecies)){
  ListData <- IrisBySpecies[[n]]
  output[[n]] <- data.frame(species=n,
                    MinPetalLength=min(ListData$Petal.Length),
                    MaxPetalLength=max(ListData$Petal.Length),
                    MeanPetalLength=mean(ListData$Petal.Length),
                    NumberofSamples=nrow(ListData))
  output.df <- do.call(rbind,output)
}
print(output.df)
```

The output is as follows:

```
> print(output.df)
           MinPetalLength MaxPetalLength MeanPetalLength NumberofSamples
setosa               1.0            1.9           1.462              50
versicolor           3.0            5.1           4.260              50
virginica            4.5            6.9           5.552              50
```

Output printout to the R Console

We used a `for` loop here, but they can be expensive in terms of processing. We can achieve the same end by using a function that uses a vector called Tapply. Tapply processes data in groups. **Tapply** has three parameters: the vector of data, the factor that defines the group, and a function. It works by extracting the group, and then applying the function to each of the groups. Then, it returns a vector with the results. We can see an example of Tapply here, using the same dataset:

```
output <-
data.frame(MinPetalLength=tapply(iris$Petal.Length,iris$Species,min),
           MaxPetalLength=tapply(iris$Petal.
Length,iris$Species,max),
```

```
                    MeanPetalLength=tapply(iris$Petal.
Length,iris$Species,mean),
                    NumberofSamples=tapply(iris$Petal.
Length,iris$Species,length))
```

```
print(output)
```

This time, we get the same output as previously. The only difference is that by using a vectorized function, we have concise code that runs efficiently.

To summarize, R is extremely flexible and it's possible to achieve the same objective in a number of different ways. As we move forward through this book, we will make recommendations about the optimal method to select, and the reasons for the recommendation.

Functions

R has many functions that are included as part of the installation. In the first instance, let's look to see how we can work smart by finding out what functions are available by default.

In our last example, we used the `split()` function. To find out more about the `split` function, we can simply use the following command:

```
?split
```

As an alternative, we can use the following statement:

```
help(split)
```

It's possible to get an overview of the arguments required for a function. To do this, simply use the `args` command:

```
args(split)
```

Fortunately, it's also possible to see examples of each function by using the following command:

```
example(split)
```

If you need more information than the documented help file about each function, you can use the following command. It will go and search through all the documentation for instances of the keyword:

```
help.search("split")
```

If you want to search the R project site from within RStudio, you can use the `RSiteSearch` command. For example:

```
RSiteSearch("split")
```

Creating your own function

There are a few important items to note about the creation of functions in R. Functions return a value. As a rule, functions return the value of the last expression in the function body.

Local variables are set temporarily for the duration of the function call, and they are cleared when the function exists.

Function parameters affect the function locally, and the original caller's value is not changed.

You can create your own functions using the `function` keyword. Here is an example of a function created from an earlier piece of code:

```
myfunction <- function(x, y, z) tapply(x,y,z)
```

So, if we take our earlier example, we could change it so that it uses functions:

```
output <-
  data.frame(MinPetalLength=myfunction(iris$Petal.
Length,iris$Species,max),
           MaxPetalLength=myfunction(iris$Petal.
Length,iris$Species,max),
           MeanPetalLength=myfunction(iris$Petal.
Length,iris$Species,mean),
           NumberofSamples=myfunction(iris$Petal.
Length,iris$Species,length))
print(output)
```

Making R run more efficiently in Tableau

It is recommended to preload R libraries before R starts. The library can be preloaded before Rserve starts by using an Rserve configuration file. It is possible to use a `library()` call in the R script, but this would mean that the library would be loaded afresh every time the view is refreshed. This is another step for the user, and we are trying to make it as simple as possible.

Summary

In this chapter, we have looked at various essential structures in working with R. We have looked at the data structures that are fundamental to using R optimally. We have also taken the view that structures such as `for` loops can often be done better as vectorized operations. Finally, we have looked at the ways in which R can be used to create functions to simplify code.

3

A Methodology for Advanced Analytics Using Tableau and R

In the era of big data when lack of methodology is likely to produce random and false discoveries, a robust framework for delivery is extremely important. According to a **Dataversity** poll in 2015, it was found that only 17% of survey respondents said they had a well-developed Predictive or Prescriptive Analytics program in place. On the other hand, 80% of respondents said they planned on implementing such a program within five years. How can we ensure that our projects are successful?

There is an increasing amount of data in the world, and in our databases. The data deluge is not going to go away anytime soon! Businesses risk wasting the useful business value of information contained in databases, unless they are able to excise useful knowledge from the data.

There is a saying in the world of data: *garbage in, garbage out*. Data needs to be cleaned before it is turned into information. There is a difference between original raw data and clean processed data, which is analysis.

It can be hard to know how to get started. Fortunately, there are a number of frameworks in data science that help us to work our way through an analytics project. Processes such as Microsoft **Team Data Science Process** (TDSP) and **CRISP-DM** position analytics as a repeatable process that is part of a bigger vision.

Why are they important? The Microsoft TDSP Process and the CRISP-DM frameworks are frameworks for analytics projects that lead to standardized delivery for organizations, both large and small.

In this chapter, we will look at these frameworks in more detail, and see how they can inform our own analytics projects and drive collaboration between teams. How can we have the analysis shaped so that it follows a pattern so that data cleansing is included?

Industry standard methodologies for analytics

There are a few main methodologies: the Microsoft TDSP Process and the CRISP-DM methodology.

Ultimately, they are all setting out to achieve the same objectives as an analytics framework. There are differences, of course, and these are highlighted here. CRISP-DM and TDSP focus on the business value and the results derived from analytics projects.

Both of these methodologies are described in the following sections.

CRISP-DM

One common methodology is the CRISP-DM methodology (the modeling agency). The **Cross Industry Standard Process for Data Mining** or (**CRISP-DM**) model as it is known, is a process model that provides a fluid framework for devising, creating, building, testing, and deploying machine learning solutions. The process is loosely divided into six main phases. The phases can be seen in the following diagram:

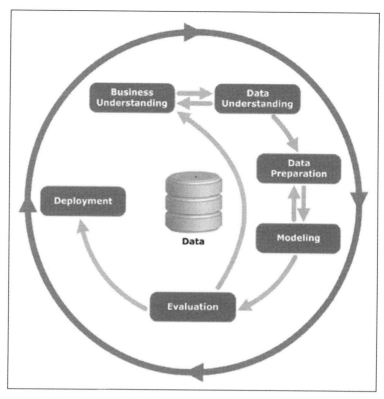

CRISP-DM Methodology

Initially, the process starts with a business idea and a general consideration of the data. Each stage is briefly discussed in the following sections.

Business understanding/data understanding

The first phase looks at the machine learning solution from a business standpoint, rather than a technical standpoint. The business idea is defined, and a draft project plan is generated. Once the business idea is defined, the data understanding phase focuses on data collection and familiarity. At this point, missing data may be identified, or initial insights may be revealed. This process feeds back to the business understanding phase.

CRISP-DM model — data preparation

In this stage, data will be cleansed and transformed, and it will be shaped ready for the modeling phase.

CRISP-DM — modeling phase

In the modeling phase, various techniques are applied to the data. The models are further tweaked and refined, and this may involve going back to the data preparation phase in order to correct any unexpected issues.

CRISP-DM — evaluation

The models need to be tested and verified to ensure that they meet the business objectives that were defined initially in the business understanding phase. Otherwise, we may have built models that do not answer the business question.

CRISP-DM — deployment

The models are published so that the customer can make use of them. This is not the end of the story, however.

CRISP-DM — process restarted

We live in a world of ever-changing data, business requirements, customer needs, and environments, and the process will be repeated.

CRISP-DM summary

CRISP-DM is the most commonly used framework for implementing machine learning projects specifically, and it applies to analytics projects as well.

It has a good focus on the business understanding piece. However, one major drawback is that the model no longer seems to be actively maintained. The official site, CRISP-DM.org, is no longer being maintained. Furthermore, the framework itself has not been updated on issues on working with new technologies, such as big data.

Big data technologies means that there can be additional effort spend in the data understanding phase, for example, as the business grapples with the additional complexities that are involved in the shape of big data sources.

The next framework, Microsoft's Team Data Science Process framework, is aimed at including big data among its data sources.

Team Data Science Process

The TDSP process model provides a dynamic framework to machine learning solutions that have been through a robust process of planning, producing, constructing, testing, and deploying models. Here is an example of the TDSP process:

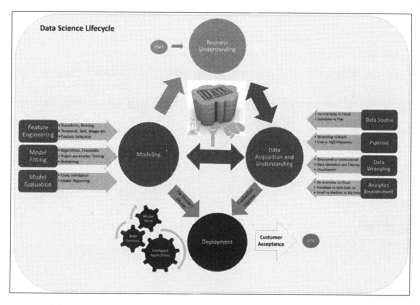

Credit: `https://docs.microsoft.com/en-us/azure/machine-learning/data-science-process-overview`

The process is loosely divided into four main phases:

- Business Understanding
- Data Acquisition and Understanding
- Modeling
- Deployment

The phases are described in the following paragraphs.

Business understanding

The Business understanding process starts with a business idea, which is solved with a machine learning solution. The business idea is defined from the business perspective, and possible scenarios are identified and evaluated. Ultimately, a project plan is generated for delivering the solution.

Data acquisition and understanding

Following on from the business understanding phase is the data acquisition and understanding phase, which concentrates on familiarity and fact-finding about the data.

The process itself is not completely linear; the output of the data acquisition and understanding phase can feed back to the business understanding phase, for example. At this point, some of the essential technical pieces start to appear, such as connecting to data, and the integration of multiple data sources. From the user's perspective, there may be actions arising from this effort. For example, it may be noted that there is missing data from the dataset, which requires further investigation before the project proceeds further.

Modeling

In the modeling phase of the TDSP process, the R model is created, built, and verified against the original business question. In light of the business question, the model needs to make sense. It should also add business value, for example, by performing better than the existing solution that was in place prior to the new R model.

This stage also involves examining key metrics in evaluating our R models, which need to be tested to ensure that the models meet the original business objectives set out in the initial business understanding phase.

Deployment

R models are published to production, once they are proven to be a fit solution to the original business question. This phase involves the creation of a strategy for ongoing review of the R model's performance as well as a monitoring and maintenance plan. It is recommended to carry out a recurrent evaluation of the deployed models. The models will live in a fluid, dynamic world of data and, over time, this environment will impact their efficacy.

The TDSP process is a cycle rather than a linear process, and it does not finish, even if the model is deployed. It is comprised of a clear structure for you to follow throughout the Data Science process, and it facilitates teamwork and collaboration along the way.

TDSP Summary

The data science unicorn does not exist; that is, the person who is equally skilled in all areas of data science, right across the board. In order to ensure successful projects where each team player contributes according to their skill set, the Team Data Science Summary is a team-oriented solution that emphasizes teamwork and collaboration throughout. It recognizes the importance of working as part of a team to deliver Data Science projects. It also offers useful information on the importance of having standardized source control and backups, which can include open source technology.

Since these methodologies both cover data preparation in detail, we will focus on data preparation for the remainder of this chapter.

Working with dirty data

The process of cleaning data involves tidying the data, which usually results in making the dataset smaller because we have cleaned out some of the dirty data. What makes data dirty?

Dirty data can be due to invalid data, which is data that is false, incomplete, or doesn't conform to the accepted standard. An example of invalid data could be formatting errors, or data that is out of an acceptable range. Invalid data could also have the wrong type. For example, the **Asterix** is invalid because the acceptable formatted data is for letters only, so it can be removed.

Dirty data can be due to missing data, which is data where no value is stored. An example of missing data is data that has not been stored due to a faulty sensor. We can see that some data is missing, so it is removed from consideration.

Dirty data could also have null values. If data has null values, then programs may respond differently to the data on that basis. The nulls will need to be considered in order to remove their impact, or they could be removed.

Dirty data could be due to duplicated data. This could occur due to invalid collection of data by a sensor, for example. Duplicated data needs to be fixed because it can increase the amount of total storage space taken up by the data.

Altogether, data can be very messy if it has any of these characteristics, and in some unfortunate cases it can have some, or even all of these characteristics. In machine learning, we need to remove the influence of dirty data because it can produce bad results.

Data quality is one of the issues that organizations can find very difficult to resolve. For some people, the reasons are technical in nature; the data can be very difficult to clean because of the technology itself. One of the most pernicious causes of poor data quality is due to process and user error.

What are the consequences of poor data quality? Simply put, it's bad for a business to have inaccurate or incomplete data. Poor data quality is ubiquitous in organizations, partly due to a breakdown in communication between CIOs and business managers.

In the following sections, we will focus on an R package known as `dplyr`.

Introduction to dplyr

What is `dplyr`? Well, `dplyr` can be perceived as a grammar of data manipulation. It has been created for the R community by *Hadley Wickham*, *Romain Francois*, and *RStudio*.

What does `dplyr` give the Tableau user? We will use `dplyr` in order to cleanse, summarize, group, chain, filter, and visualize our data in Tableau.

Summarizing the data with dplyr

Firstly, let's import the packages that we need. These packages are listed in the following table, followed by the code itself.

Packages required for the hands-on exercise:

Package Name	Description	Reference
WDI	Search, extract, and format data from the World Bank's World Development Indicators	`https://cran.r-project.org/web/packages/WDI/index.html`
dplyr	dplyr is a grammar of data manipulation	

As we walk through the script, the first thing we need to do is install the packages.

Once you have installed the packages, we need to call each library.

Once we have called the libraries, then we need to obtain the data from the World Data Bank website. When we have downloaded the data, we can assign it to a variable. In this example, we will call the variable `dat`. Before we do any further analysis, we will summarize the data using the `summary` command.

To start working with the data, let's use the `summary` command. In this example, the `summary` command is given here:

```
summary(dat)
```

In the next step, let's use the `head` command in order to see some of the data. Here is the command:

```
head(dat)
```

With the `dplyr` package, we can filter data so that we only see the data that we would like to see. For example, for the **World Development Indicators (WDI)** data, we may wish to see data that is labeled for the whole world. This means that it would match the word `WORLD`. In the next command, we can see the filtered data. The `filter` command looks for data that matches the condition in the code. In this example, the data is scanned for rows where the region is shown to be set to world:

```
dat[dat$Major.area..region..country.or.area.. == "WORLD"]
```

When we use the `slice` command, we can see that the data is shown for the rows that you specify in the command line.

This means that we can slice this data so that it only shows data that appears within the number of rows by position. In this example, we restrict the `slice` command so that it shows only the first three lines of code. The `slice` command is nice and neat. In contrast, if we were to rewrite the `slice` command into the corresponding command in R, the command would be less readable and it would be much longer.

We can also reorder data by using the `arrange` command. This piece of code will order the data along the lines of the columns that is stated in the function's arguments. So, for example, the following code will reorder the data using the `Country.code` column:

```
arrange(dat, Country.code)
```

We can also choose columns by using the `select` command. This command specifies which columns we would like to return. It allows us to rename the column names using variables, using the named arguments specified in the piece of code. Here is an example, where some of the column names are renamed.

However, the `select` command drops all the variables that are not explicitly stated in the code. Unfortunately, this renders the `select` command to be not that useful. Instead, we can use the `rename` command to achieve the same thing as the `select` command, but the variables are all retained, whether they are explicitly stated or not. Here is an example of the rename command in use:

```
rename(dat,Index =Index,Variant=Variant,region=Major.area..region..
country.or.area.., Notes=Notes, Countrycode=Country.code )
```

The `select` command is very useful when it is combined with the `distinct` command. The `distinct` command is designed to return the unique values in a data frame. The `select` command is used to retrieve data for the specified columns, and it is combined with the `distinct` command to return the unique values for the `selected` columns in a data frame. Here is an example where we use the `select` and `distinct` commands together, and the results are assigned to a variable called `sampledat`:

```
sampledat <- distinct(select(dat,Index,Variant,region=Major.area..
region..country.or.area.., Notes, Countrycode=Country.code, X2015=X2015,
X2016=X2016, X2017=X2017 ) )
```

Let's take a look at the output of the `sampledat` variable using the head command:

```
head(sampledat)
```

	Index	Variant	region	Notes	Countrycode	X2015	X2016	X2017
1	1	Low variant	WORLD		900	7 349 472	7 424 524	7 495 450
2	2	Low variant	More developed regions	a	901	1 251 351	1 253 385	1 254 823
3	3	Low variant	Less developed regions	b	902	6 098 121	6 171 139	6 240 627
4	4	Low variant	Least developed countries	c	941	954 158	975 701	997 132
5	5	Low variant	Less developed regions, excluding least developed countries	d	934	5 143 963	5 195 438	5 243 495
6	6	Low variant	Less developed regions, excluding China		948	4 690 815	4 759 025	4 824 738

Output of sample data

Now, let's repeat the command for the first 20 years in the dataset, from 2015 until 2035. To do this, we will execute a piece of code, which does the following things:

It selects the relevant columns, and renames some of the columns so that they are more readable. The `year` column names are renamed to remove the letter X prefix, and the year names are turned into characters by virtue of being enclosed in quotation marks. Then, the code assigns the result to a variable called `distinctdat`:

```
distinctdat <- distinct(select(dat,Index=Index,Variant=Variant,Region=Maj
or.area..region..country.or.area.., Notes, Countrycode=Country.code,

"2015"=X2015, "2016"=X2016,"2017"=X2017,"2018"=X2018,"2019"=X2019,"2020"
=X2020,

"2021"=X2021,"2022"=X2022,"2023"=X2023,"2024"=X2024,"2025"=X2025,"2026"=X
2026,"2027"=X2027,"2028"=X2028,"2029"=X2029,
```

```
"2030"=X2030,"2031"=X2031,"2032"=X2032,"2033"=X2033,"2034"=X2034,"2035"
=X2035))
```

Let's take a look at the resulting data, which is stored in the `distinctdat` variable, using the previous `head` command:

```
head(distinctdat)
```

This is an excerpt of the result set, contained in the `distinctdat` variable:

```
> head(distinctdat)
  Index    Variant                                              Region Notes Countrycode       2015
1     1 Low variant                                              WORLD                   900  7 349 472  7
2     2 Low variant                             More developed regions     a             901  1 251 351  1
3     3 Low variant                             Less developed regions     b             902  6 098 121  6
4     4 Low variant                           Least developed countries   c             941      954 158
5     5 Low variant Less developed regions, excluding least developed countries  d        934  5 143 963  5
6     6 Low variant            Less developed regions, excluding China           948  4 690 815  4
       2025       2026       2027       2028       2029       2030       2031       2032      2033      2034
```

Result set showing erroneous data format

In the column headed 2015, it's possible to see that the values contain spaces. If we were to write this data to a CSV file, only the numbers after the space would be written to the file. This means that we will need to do something about the spaces before that point.

We could use a substitution command, such as `gsub`, to remove the spaces for every year, from 2015 right through to 2035. However, this would mean repeating the command for each year. We could also write a function for this purpose, and call it for every year.

Although this method would work, the resulting data would not appear nicely in Tableau. The reason for this is that each year is still treated separately, even though the actual metric is the same. Ideally, it's better to unpivot the data.

Unpivoting columns creates an `attribute` column for each selected column heading and a `value` column for each column cell value. The attribute-value pair columns are inserted after the last column. In R, we can unpivot data using the melt command.

In our example, we would like to unpivot the data held in the `distinctdat` variable along the attribute columns, which are `Index`, `Variant`, `Region`, `Notes`, and `Countrycode`. The other rows, which hold the data from 2015 to the year 2035, would all be placed into two columns. One column will hold the year, and the other column will hold the value of the projected world population. This unpivot result is achieved with the following code:

```
melteddata <- melt(distinctdat, id=c("Index","Variant","Region","Notes","
Countrycode"))
```

In the preceding example, each date column becomes a row with an `attribute` column containing the date value and a `value` column containing the date column value. So, if we run the preceding command, then data is stored in the `melteddata` variable.

If we `slice` the `melteddata` variable, then we can see the results more clearly:

	Index	Variant	Region	Notes	Countrycode	variable	value
1	1	Low variant	WORLD		900	2015	7 349 472
2	2	Low variant	More developed regions	a	901	2015	1 251 351
3	3	Low variant	Less developed regions	b	902	2015	6 098 121
4	4	Low variant	Least developed countries	c	941	2015	954 158
5	5	Low variant	Less developed regions, excluding least developed countries	d	934	2015	5 143 963
6	6	Low variant	Less developed regions, excluding China		948	2015	4 690 815
7	7	Low variant	High-income countries	e	1503	2015	1 401 479
8	8	Low variant	Middle-income countries	e	1517	2015	5 306 283
9	9	Low variant	Upper-middle-income countries	e	1502	2015	2 390 125
10	10	Low variant	Lower-middle-income countries	e	1501	2015	2 916 158

From the preceding example code output, we can see that the `year` data now appears in the **variable** column. The population count data is now held in the **value** column.

Now it's possible to work with the value column in order to remove the spaces. Before we do that, let's tidy up the column names so that further code will be more readable.

Since we looked at rename earlier, let's look at a different way of achieving the same thing, whilst showing the different functionality of `dplyr`. We can add a new `year` column, to hold the `year` data. Also, we can add a new column called `populationcount`, which is a duplicate of the **value** column. We can do this simply by running the following commands to create new columns:

```
melteddata$PopulationCount <- melteddata$value
```

```
melteddata$Year <- melteddata$variable
```

Then, we can use the select command in `dplyr` to select the rest of the columns, removing the value column:

```
melteddata <- select(melteddata, select=-value, -variable)
```

This piece of code means that all of the columns held in the `melteddata` variable are selected except the value and variable columns, which are denoted with the minus in front of them. The remaining columns are assigned to the `melteddata` variable. We can use the `slice` command again to see what's contained in the `melteddata` variable, and you can see an example output as follows:

Index	Variant	Region	Notes	Countrycode	Year	PopulationCount
1	1 Low variant	WORLD		900	2015	7 349 472
2	2 Low variant	More developed regions	a	901	2015	1 251 351
3	3 Low variant	Less developed regions	b	902	2015	6 098 121
4	4 Low variant	Least developed countries	c	941	2015	954 158
5	5 Low variant	Less developed regions, excluding least developed countries	d	934	2015	5 143 963
6	6 Low variant	Less developed regions, excluding China		948	2015	4 690 815
7	7 Low variant	High-income countries	e	1503	2015	1 401 479
8	8 Low variant	Middle-income countries	e	1517	2015	5 306 283
9	9 Low variant	Upper-middle-income countries	e	1502	2015	2 390 125
10	10 Low variant	Lower-middle-income countries	e	1501	2015	2 916 158

Renamed output

Let's move forward to work with the `PopulationCount` data, so that we can remove the spaces. In order to do that, we will use the `gsub` pattern matching and replacement mechanism. The `gsub` function replaces all occurrences of a particular pattern in a string.

In order to use `gsub`, we have to specify that the data is a factor. The following code takes care of the conversion:

```
melteddata$PopulationCount <- as.factor(melteddata$PopulationCount)
```

The piece of code `as.factor` does the conversion part. It is more efficient than using strings. Factors can be used in statistical modeling, where they will be assigned the correct number of the degrees of freedom. Factors are also very useful when we are working with graphics in Tableau, because they will be easy for the business users to understand and use in their own analyses. As before, the new data is assigned to the old variable name.

In the following piece of code, we will use `gsub` for the substitution process. It will replace every instance of a space with nothing, thereby removing the spaces. Then, the changes will be assigned back to the `PopulationCount` column. The code is given as follows:

```
melteddata$PopulationCount <- gsub(" ","",melteddata$PopulationCount)
```

Once the spaces have been removed, let's change the data type back so that it is a numeric data type. Down the line, this means that the output is more likely to be recognized as a number by Tableau. For users, it will be easier for them to work with the data if it is presented to them conveniently, so that they can start to get insights at the earliest. Although Tableau makes it easy for business users to change data types, users prefer not to have any impedance in their way when working with data. The command is as follows:

```
melteddata$PopulationCount <- as.numeric(melteddata$PopulationCount)
```

We can slice the data again, in order to see how it looks now:

	Index	Variant	Region	Notes	Countrycode	Year	PopulationCount
1	1	Low variant	WORLD		900	2015	7349472
2	2	Low variant	More developed regions	a	901	2015	1251351
3	3	Low variant	Less developed regions	b	902	2015	6098121
4	4	Low variant	Least developed countries	c	941	2015	954158
5	5	Low variant	Less developed regions, excluding least developed countries	d	934	2015	5143963
6	6	Low variant	Less developed regions, excluding China		948	2015	4690815
7	7	Low variant	High-income countries	e	1503	2015	1401479
8	8	Low variant	Middle-income countries	e	1517	2015	5306283
9	9	Low variant	Upper-middle-income countries	e	1502	2015	2390125
10	10	Low variant	Lower-middle-income countries	e	1501	2015	2916158

Completed dataset

Once we have fixed our data, we can look at other activities on the data, such as grouping the data. We can use the `summarise` command in order to group the data. In this example, we are grouping the data so that we have the overall population mean. We have a variable called `OverallPopulationmean`, and it contains the overall count of rows, along with the mean of population. Here is the example code:

```
OverallPopulationmean <- summarise(melteddata, count=n(),
                            OverallPopulationmean = mean(melteddat
a$PopulationCount, na.rm=TRUE))
```

The result is given here:

```
  count OverallPopulationmean
1  5733              249386.9
```

However, this isn't an accurate picture, because we know that the data itself contains both summary and detail data. Let's write the data to a CSV file, and we can explore it further in Tableau:

```
write.csv(melteddata, "melteddata.csv")
```

When we import the cleansed data into Tableau, we can filter the data so that we can simply see the **Region** data. Here is an example worksheet:

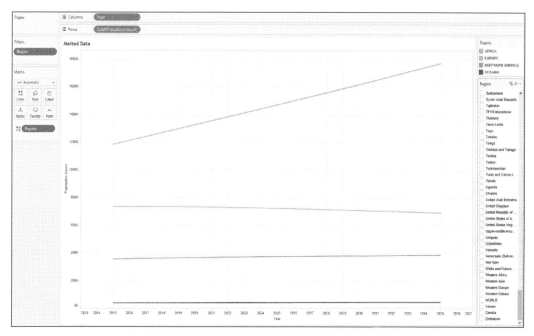

Sample Tableau Workbook with cleansed data

We have nice, clean line charts, which explain the message of the data. According to the projections, there is a steep projected rise in **Africa**, with a slight fall off in Europe.

What would happen if we hadn't cleansed the data? Well, let's give Tableau the dirty dataset, and let's see what happens.

We can import the CSV file straight from the World Data Bank website, and into Tableau. The first thing that we notice is that instead of having a nice **Year** dimension, all of the years appear as individual dimensions. Here is an example:

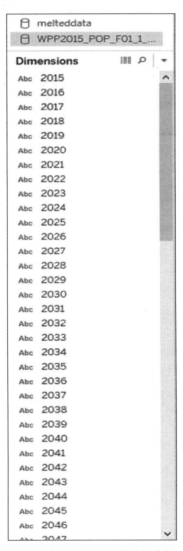

Tableau import of the Years as individual dimensions

Unfortunately, this makes the data very difficult to navigate. The Tableau user would have to **drag** each **year** to the canvas. In the following example, let's take across the years from 2015 to 2030. Now let's see what happens:

Dirty Data											2025 / 2026 / 2027 / 2028 / 2029 / 2030				
	.. 1, 1, 1, 1	.28, 1 233	..96, 1 418	.. 472 568	.. 251 616	..75, 1 273	..92, 1 400	.. 426 454	..55, 1 246	..54, 1 349	.. 385 587	..29, 1 540	.. 425 862	.. 617 191
	1	1 236	1 439	1 501 512	1 249 703	1 270	1 408	1 434 957	1 238	1 344	1 382 791	1 551	1 425 894	1 613 517
	1	1 240	1 461	1 530 541	1 247 507	1 267	1 416	1 442 923	1 229	1 339	1 379 485	1 561	1 425 575	1 609 275
	1	1 244	1 482	1 559 735	1 245 082	1 263	1 423	1 450 425	1 219	1 333	1 375 746	1 570	1 424 964	1 604 549
	1	1 247	1 503	1 589 196	1 242 489	1 260	1 430	1 457 560	1 210	1 326	1 371 660	1 579	1 424 135	1 599 436
Major area, r..	1	1 250	1 524	1 618 995	1 239 777	1 256	1 437	1 464 395	1 201	1 320	1 367 292	1 588	1 423 142	1 594 009
Afghanistan														
AFRICA				Abc										
Albania														
Algeria														
American Sa..														
Andorra														
Angola														
Anguilla														
Antigua and ..														
Argentina														
Armenia														
Aruba														
ASIA														
Australia														
Australia/Ne..														
Austria														
Azerbaijan														
Bahamas														
Bahrain												Abc		
Bangladesh														
Barbados														
Belarus														
Belgium														
Belize														

Tableau import of the dirty data

We can see here that the results are almost impossible for Tableau to visualize. The data is difficult for Tableau to interpret, and this result isn't going to be a good experience for the end users.

Summary

Data science requires a process to ensure that the project is successful. As we have seen from the previous frameworks, it requires many moving parts from the extraction of timely data from diverse data sources, building and testing the models, and then deploying those models to aid in or to automate day-to-day decision making processes. Otherwise, the project can easily fall through the gaps in this data so that the organization is right where they started: data rich, information poor.

In this example, we have covered the CRISP-DM methodology and the TDSP methodology. Each of these stages has the data preparation stage clearly marked out. In order to follow this sequence, we have started with a focus on the data preparation stage using the `dplyr` package in R. We have cleaned some data and compared the results between the dirty and clean data.

4
Prediction with R and Tableau Using Regression

In this chapter, we will consider regression from an analytics point of view. We will look at the predictive capabilities and performance of regression algorithms, which is a great start for the analytics program. At the end of this chapter, you'll have experience in simple linear regression, multi-linear regression, and k-Nearest Neighbors regression using a business-oriented understanding of the actual use cases of the regression techniques.

We will focus on preparing, exploring, and modeling the data in R, combined with the visualization power of Tableau in order to express the findings in the data.

Some interesting datasets come from the UCI machine learning datasets, which can be obtained from the following link: `https://archive.ics.uci.edu/ml/datasets.html`.

During the course of this chapter, we will use datasets that are obtained from the UCI website, in addition to default R datasets.

Getting started with regression

Regression means the unbiased prediction of the conditional expected value, using independent variables, and the dependent variable. A dependent variable is the variable that we want to predict. Examples of a dependent variable could be a number such as price, sales, or weight. An independent variable is a characteristic, or feature, that helps to determine the dependent variable. So, for example, the independent variable of weight could help to determine the dependent variable of weight.

Regression analysis can be used in forecasting, time series modeling, and cause and effect relationships.

Simple linear regression

R can help us to build prediction stories with Tableau. Linear regression is a great starting place when you want to predict a number, such as profit, cost, or sales. In simple linear regression, there is only one independent variable x, which predicts a dependent value, y.

Simple linear regression is usually expressed with a line that identifies the slope that helps us to make predictions. So, if *sales* = x and *profit* = y, what is the slope that allows us to make the prediction? We will do this in R to create the calculation, and then we will repeat it in R. We can also color-code it so that we can see what is above and what is below the slope.

Using lm() to conduct a simple linear regression

What is linear regression? Linear regression has the objective if finding a model that fits a regression line through the data well, whilst reducing the discrepancy, or error, between the data and the regression line. If the regression model is significant, it will be able to account for the error, and the regression line will fit the data better because it will minimize the error. The error is also known as the residuals, and it is measured as the sum of squared errors of error, which is sometimes abbreviated to SSE. It is calculated as the model's deviations predicted from actual empirical values of data. In practice, a small error amount, or SSE, indicates that the data is a close match to the model.

 In order to do regression, we need to measure the y distance of each of the points from a line of best fit and then sum the error margin (that is, the distance to the line).

We are trying to predict the line of best fit between one or many variables from a scatter plot of points of data. To find the line of best fit, we need to calculate a couple of things about the line. We can use the `lm()` function to obtain the line, which we can call m:

- We need to calculate the slope of the line m
- We also need to calculate the intercept with the y axis c

So we begin with the equation of the line:

$$y = mx + c$$

To get the line, we use the concept of **Ordinary Least Squares (OLS)**. This means that we sum the square of the y-distances between the points and the line. Furthermore, we can rearrange the formula to give us beta (or *m*) in terms of the number of points *n*, *x*, and *y*. This would assume that we can minimize the mean error with the line and the points. It will be the best predictor for all of the points in the training set and future feature vectors.

Let's start with a simple example in R, where we predict women's weight from their height. If we were articulating this question per Microsoft's Team Data Science Process, we would be stating this as a business question during the *business understanding* phase. How can we come up with a model that helps us to predict what the women's weight is going to be, dependent on their height?

Using this business question as a basis for further investigation, how do we come up with a model from the data, which we could then use for further analysis? Simple linear regression is about two variables, an independent and a dependent variable, which is also known as the predictor variable. With only one variable, and no other information, the best prediction is the mean of the sample itself. In other words, when all we have is one variable, the mean is the best predictor of any one amount. The first step is to collect a random sample of data. In R, we are lucky to have sample data that we can use.

To explore linear regression, we will use the women dataset, which is installed by default with R. The variability of the weight amount can only be explained by the weights themselves, because that is all we have.

To conduct the regression, we will use the lm function, which appears as follows:

```
model <- lm(y ~ x, data=mydata)
```

To see the women dataset, open up RStudio. When we type in the variable name, we will get the contents of the variable. In this example, the variable name women will give us the data itself.

The women's height and weight are printed out to the console, and here is an example:

```
> women
```

When we type in this variable name, we get the actual data itself, which we can see next:

height <dbl>	weight <dbl>
58	115
59	117
60	120
61	123
62	126
63	129
64	132
65	135
66	139
67	142

1-10 of 15 rows

We can visualize the data quite simply in R, using the `plot(women)` command. The plot command provides a quick and easy way of visualizing the data. Our objective here is simply to see the relationship of the data.

The results appear as follows:

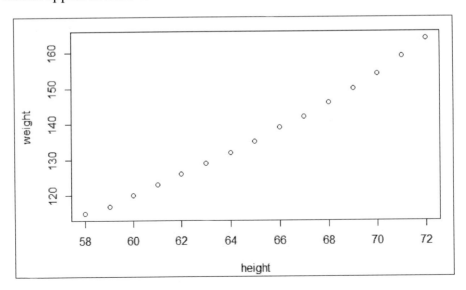

Now that we can see the relationship of the data, we can use the summary command to explore the data further:

```
summary(women)
```

This will give us the results, which are given here as follows:

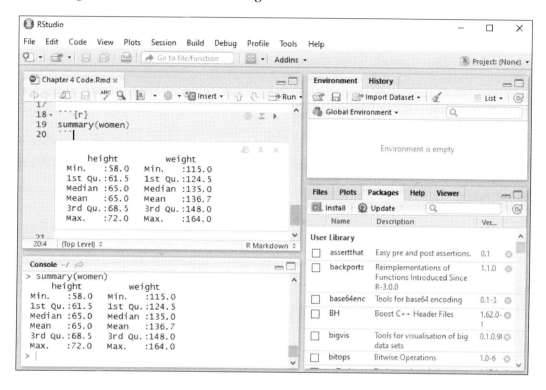

Let's look at the results in closer detail:

```
          height            weight
 Min.    :58.0    Min.     :115.0
 1st Qu.:61.5    1st Qu.:124.5
 Median :65.0    Median :135.0
 Mean    :65.0    Mean     :136.7
 3rd Qu.:68.5    3rd Qu.:148.0
 Max.    :72.0    Max.     :164.0
```

Next, we can create a model that will use the `lm` function to create a linear regression model of the data. We will assign the results to a model called `linearregressionmodel`, as follows:

```r
linearregressionmodel <- lm(weight ~ height, data=women)
```

What does the model produce? We can use the summary command again, and this will provide some descriptive statistics about the lm model that we have generated. One of the nice, understated features of R is its ability to use variables. Here we have our variable, `linearregressionmodel` – note that one word is storing a whole model!

```r
summary(linearregressionmodel)
```

How does this appear in the R interface? Here is an example:

```
Chapter 4 Code.Rmd

22
23  ```{r}
24  linearregressionmodel <- lm(weight ~ height, data=women)
25
26  ```
27  ```{r}
28  summary(linearregressionmodel)
29  ```

Call:
lm(formula = weight ~ height, data = women)

Residuals:
    Min      1Q  Median      3Q     Max
-1.7333 -1.1333 -0.3833  0.7417  3.1167

Coefficients:
             Estimate Std. Error t value Pr(>|t|)
(Intercept) -87.51667    5.93694  -14.74 1.71e-09 ***
height        3.45000    0.09114   37.85 1.09e-14 ***
---
Signif. codes:  0 '***' 0.001 '**' 0.01 '*' 0.05 '.' 0.1 ' ' 1

Residual standard error: 1.525 on 13 degrees of freedom
Multiple R-squared:  0.991,    Adjusted R-squared:  0.9903
F-statistic:  1433 on 1 and 13 DF,  p-value: 1.091e-14
```

What do these numbers mean? Let's take a closer look at some of the key numbers.

Coefficients

What are coefficients? It means that one change in x causes an expected change in y. Here is how it looks in R:

```
Coefficients:
              Estimate
(Intercept) -87.51667
height        3.45000
```

We can see that the values of coefficients are given as -87.51667 and 3.45000. It means that one unit change in x, the weight, causes a -87.51667 unit change in the expected value of y, the height.

If we were to write this as an equation, the general model could be written as follows:

$y = a + b\,x$

This means that our prediction equation for the `linearregressionmodel` model is as follows:

```
Linearregressionmodel = -87.52 + (3.45 * height)
```

We can get this information another way in R. We can see the coefficients by simply using the variable name `linearregressionmodel`, which outputs the result as follows:

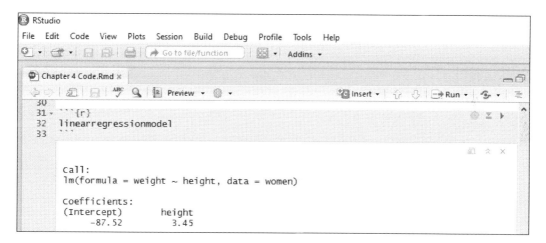

Residual standard error

In the output, residual standard error is cost, which is *1.525*.

Comparing actual values with predicted results

Now, we will look at real values of weight of 15 women first and then will look at predicted values. Actual values of weight of 15 women are as follows, using the following command:

```
women$weight
```

When we execute the women$weight command, this is the result that we obtain:

```
> women$weight
 [1] 115 117 120 123 126 129 132 135 139 142 146 150 154 159 164
```

When we look at the predicted values, these are also read out in R:

```
> linearregressionmodel$fitted.values
       1        2        3        4        5        6        7        8
112.5833 116.0333 119.4833 122.9333 126.3833 129.8833 133.2833 136.7333
       9       10       11       12       13       14       15
140.1833 143.6333 147.0833 150.5333 153.9833 157.4333 160.8833
```

How can we put these pieces of data together?

```
women$pred <- linearregressionmodel$fitted.values
```

This is a very simple merge. When we look inside the women variable again, this is the result:

	height	weight	pred
1	58	115	112.5833
2	59	117	116.0333
3	60	120	119.4833
4	61	123	122.9333
5	62	126	126.3833
6	63	129	129.8833
7	64	132	133.2833
8	65	135	136.7333
9	66	139	140.1833
10	67	142	143.6333
11	68	146	147.0833
12	69	150	150.5333
13	70	154	153.9833
14	71	159	157.4333
15	72	164	160.8833

Investigating relationships in the data

We can see the column names in the model by using the `names` command. In our example, it will appear as follows:

```
names(linearregressionmodel)
```

When we use this command, we get the following columns:

```
[1]  "coefficients"  "residuals"      "effects"
[4]  "rank"          "fitted.values" "assign"
[7]  "qr"            "df.residual"   "xlevels"
[10] "call"          "terms"          "model"
```

We can identify the relationship between height and weight, by calculating the correlation. To do this, we can use **Pearson's correlation coefficient**, which is a measure of the linear correlation between two variables X and Y. It produces a result in the form of a value between *+1* and *−a* inclusive, where *1* is a total positive correlation, *0* is no correlation, and *-1* shows a perfect negative correlation. This value is known as **Pearson's R**.

In this example, we can use the `cor` function to compute Pearson's correlation coefficient. In our example, it appears as follows:

```
rmodel <- cor(weight,height)
```

We can see the result of the model by using the following command:

```
rmodel^2
```

We get the result of Pearson's R as follows:

```
0.9910098
```

This shows a high positive correlation between `height` and `weight`. We can find out more information by using the `plot` command, which will provide us with four visualizations in R. The command appears as follows:

```
plot(linearregression)
```

In order to assess the efficiency of the model in explaining the data, R provides us with four plots, which are tabulated as follows:

Plot Name	Purpose	Sample Plot
Residuals versus Leverage	This is a measure of the importance of determining the regression result. Cook's distance measures the importance of each observation to the regression line. Large distances indicate an outlier.	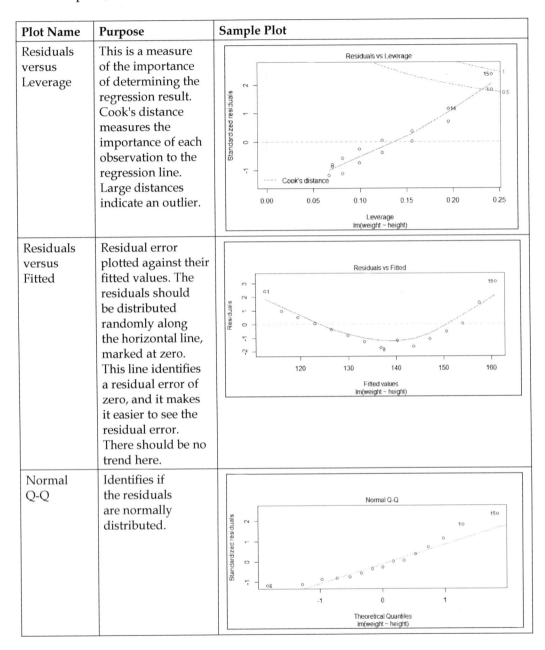
Residuals versus Fitted	Residual error plotted against their fitted values. The residuals should be distributed randomly along the horizontal line, marked at zero. This line identifies a residual error of zero, and it makes it easier to see the residual error. There should be no trend here.	
Normal Q-Q	Identifies if the residuals are normally distributed.	

Plot Name	Purpose	Sample Plot
Scale-Location	This shows the square root of the relative error. There should be no trend here.	

Replicating our results using R and Tableau together

In this topic, let's get to work! Now that we have done some analysis and data visualisation in R, we will replicate our results using R and Tableau together.

Abc women.csv index	# women.csv Height	# women.csv Weight	# women.csv Pred
1	58	115	112.5833
2	59	117	116.0333
3	60	120	119.4833
4	61	123	122.9333
5	62	126	126.3833
6	63	129	129.8333
7	64	132	133.2833
8	65	135	136.7333

In the screenshot, we can see the index, original height, and original weight along with the Predicted amount. In the first row, we can see that the weight was 115 pounds, and the predicted amount was 112.6 pounds.

In Tableau, the calculation is gained using the **Calculation Editor**. An example is shown in the following screenshot:

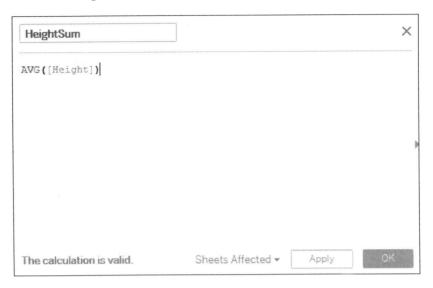

As we have done with height, we are also going to going to create the calculation for weight as seen in the following screenshot:

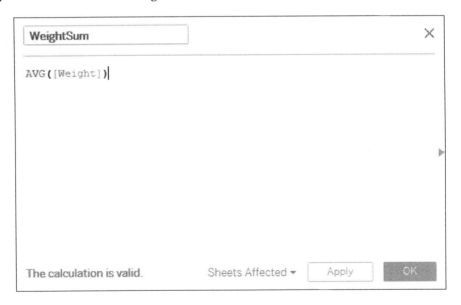

When these calculated fields have been created, you can create the calculated field that holds the R calculation. The following screenshot will show a diagram of this field:

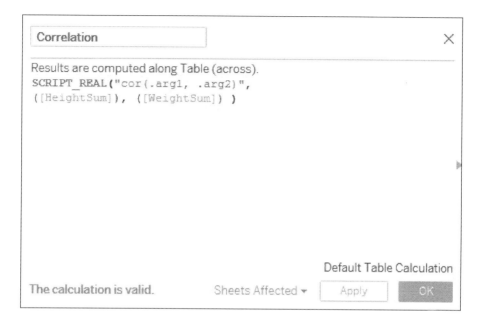

Once the calculated fields have been created, you can drag the fields onto the canvas.

So we can calculate the correlation for all the fields, we need an index. Move index to the **Dimensions** tab by dragging it up from the **Measures** tab:

```
Create a formula for R
SCRIPT_REAL("cor(.arg1, .arg2)",
([HeightSum]), ([WeightSum]) )
```

- Then, drag HeightSum to Columns.
- Next, drag WeightSum to Rows.
- To show all of the marks, Add Index to the Detail Mark.

- Add Correlation to the Detail Mark. Here is an example:

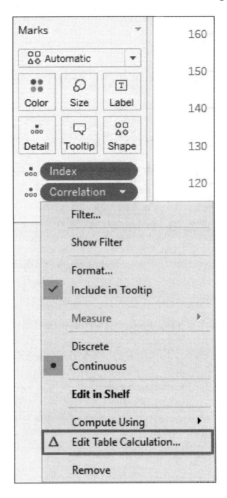

When we look to see what the Correlation field is showing now, we can see that it isn't holding anything. How can we resolve that issue? Now, we need to fix the calculated field holding the R formula. It will need to be configured to show the correct settings for the calculation.

Our correlation is happening at the table level. However, in order to ensure that all data points are included in the correlation, we are going to specify here that the **Index** column is included. This means that all data points are included. Here is an example:

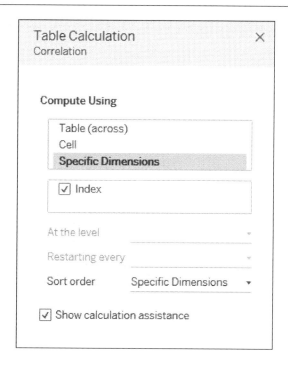

Once we have done all of these steps, we can see that the **Correlation** field is now populated with a very high population.

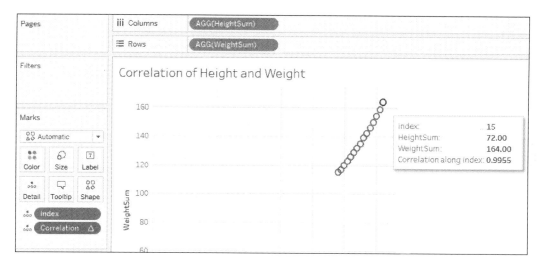

Getting started with multiple regression?

Simple linear regression will summarize the relationship between an outcome and a single explanatory element. However, in real life, things are not always so simple! We are going to use the adult dataset from UCI, which focuses on census data with a view to identifying if adults earn above or below fifty thousand dollars a year. The idea is that we can build a model from observations of adult behavior, to see if the individuals earn above or below fifty thousand dollars a year.

Multiple regression builds a model of the data, which is used to make predictions. Multiple regression is a scoring model, which makes a summary. It predicts a value between *0* and *1*, which means that it is good for predicting probabilities.

It's possible to imagine multiple regression as modeling the behavior of a coin being tossed in the air. How will the coin land—heads or tails? It is not dependent on just one thing. The reality is that the result will depend on other variables. This score is the probability of the result. In other words, the result of the coin face being heads depends on the other variables, and this score is expressed as a probability. The probability is the resulting, predicted number, which is an additive function of the inputs. The resulting model also gives an indication of the relative impact of each input variable on the output.

Building our multiple regression model

The first thing we need to do in the model building process is to select a dataset—this should be something that contains a fairly large number of samples (observations). We have selected some datasets here as examples.

Once the dataset has been selected, we want to ensure that we can use the dataset to determine something about the business question that we are trying to answer. We are trying to make predictions on the data, so our training set should be in the same shape as the test dataset. A feature is an item that can be used to predict a value in an experiment.

Once we have built our model, we can accurately test the predictions and see whether our guesses are accurate and then rank the efficiency of our model. At the end of this process, we can evaluate the model and determine whether this is a good fit or not. Ultimately, this could mean changing the way we interact with our data, or perhaps amending the algorithm we use to optimize the efficiency of the model.

When we trained our model, we only selected the greater proportion of the dataset. In fact, we can use the rest of the dataset to test whether we can accurately predict a value, and this is the test dataset.

Supervised learning is distinct from unsupervised learning, which we'll look at later on in this book. In the domain of supervised learning, we try to predict either a continuous variable, a number, for example, a predicted earning level for adults and other conditions or a class of output that is discrete, such as earning level. In order to do this task, we need two things:

- The first is features—these will need to be in a form that our machine learning algorithm can process. The mathematical term for this is a vector—so we refer to this as a feature vector.

- We also need a set of labels—these are generally in text form, but we may need them to be in numeric form, so as part of the input we may have to turn them into a set of numbers that our algorithm can understand.

Once we have our features vectors and labels we can feed these into an algorithm that will attempt to build a model from the input data

The algorithm produces a training set from part of our input dataset and we can refer to the trained model now—it is important to understand that the model can be continually trained as we discover new things and get new data—machine learning is so powerful because of the feedback cycle involved.

Is the model good or bad? How do we evaluate a regression model?

Confusion matrix

One way of doing this is to build in a confusion matrix from the result. A confusion matrix is a very simple and precise way of summarizing the result. The confusion matrix is a simple table that shows the actual classification against the predicted ones.

It will be built from a particular class—in this case, *Iris Versicolor*.

Starting from the top, we derived the following:

- 12 true positives—this means we accurately predicted *Iris Versicolor* 12 times

- Three false positives—this means that we labeled *Iris Setosa* and *Iris Virginica* incorrectly as *Iris Versicolor* three times

- Six false negatives—this is the *Iris Versicolor* that were incorrectly marked as the other two types

- Nine true negatives—this is the remaining classes that were classified correctly as non-*Iris Versicolor* types

In the next example, we will see an example of this scenario in R, and then we can visualize the results in Tableau.

Prerequisites

The following items are prerequisites for the exercise:

- Tableau 10
- Adult UCI data, which you can obtain from `https://archive.ics.uci.edu/ml/datasets/Adult`
- R and RStudio

Instructions

In order to proceed, you will need to download the data as follows:

1. Download the CSV file containing the adult UCI data.

2. You will need to do this for the test and also for training data.

3. For the test data, the link is here: `https://archive.ics.uci.edu/ml/machine-learning-databases/adult/adult.test`.

4. For the training data, the link is here: `https://archive.ics.uci.edu/ml/machine-learning-databases/adult/adult.data`.

5. Load the CSV file into R, and assign it to the adult variable name. Your code could look like the following segment:

   - `adult.training | read.csv (C:/Users/jenst/Downloads/adult.csv)`

   - `adult.test | read.csv (C:/Users/jenst/Downloads/adulttest.csv)`

6. Let's create a binary response variable called y, which will be our dependent variable. It is based on the number of records in the training dataset:

   ```
   N.obs <- dim(adult.training) [1]
   y <- rep(0, N.obs)


   y[class==levels(class) [2]] <- 1
   ```

7. Next, we will look at the columns in the dataset, using the `summary` command:

   ```
   summary(adult.training)
   ```

8. We can use the `names` command to obtain the column name:

   ```
   names(adult.training)
   ```

9. We can also view some of the data in R, using the `head` command:

    ```
    head(adult.training)
    ```

10. Now, we will use the `glm` function in order to create a data model, which we will assign to the `adultdatamodel` variable:

    ```
    ## GLM fit
    adultdatamodel <- glm(y ~ age + educationnum + hoursperweek +
    workclass + maritalstatus + occupation + relationship + race +
    sex, family=binomial("logit"))
    ```

11. Once we have obtained the result, we need to check the coefficients, and we will set the results to the tab variable:

    ```
    resultstable <- summary(fit)$coefficients
    sorter <- order(resultstable[,4])
    resultstable <- resultstable[sorter,]
    ```

12. Now, we can move onto the test data, which is assigned to the `pred` variable:

    ```
    pred <- predict(fit, test.data, type="response")
    N.test <- length(pred)
    ```

13. Next we will use *0.5* as a threshold for the prediction to be successful:

    ```
    y.hat <- rep(0, N.test)
    y.hat[pred>=0.5] <- 1
    ```

14. We can visualize the data in a confusion.table in order to identify the true outcome versus the predicted outcome:

    ```
    ## Get the true outcome of the test data
    outcome <- levels(test.data$class)
    y.test <- rep(0, N.test)
    y.test[test.data$class==outcome[2]] <- 1

    confusion.table <- table(y.hat, y.test)
    colnames(confusion.table) <- c(paste("Actual",outcome[1]),
    outcome[2])
    rownames(confusion.table) <- c(paste("Predicted",outcome[1]),
    outcome[2])
    ```

Once we have our confusion table, we can print it out to a CSV file so that we can visualize it in Tableau.

Solving the business question

What are we trying to do with regression? If you are trying to solve a business question that helps predict probabilities or scoring, then regression is a great place to start. Business problems that require scoring are also known as regression problems. In this example, we have scored the likelihood of the individual earning above or below fifty thousand dollars per annum.

The main objective is to create a model that we can use on other data, too. The output is a set of results, but it is also an equation that describes the relationship between a number of predictor variables and the response variable.

What do the terms mean?

For example, you could try to estimate the probability that a given person earns above or below fifty thousand dollars:

- **Error**: The difference between predicted value and true value
- **Residuals**: The residuals are the difference between the actual values of the variable you're predicting and predicted values from your regression--$y - \hat{y}$

For most regressions, ideally, we want the residuals to look like a normal distribution when plotted. If our residuals are normally distributed, this indicates the mean of the difference between our predictions and the actual values is close to 0 (good) and that when we miss, we're missing both short and long of the actual value, and the likelihood of a miss being far from the actual value gets smaller as the distance from the actual value gets larger.

Think of it like a dartboard. A good model is going to hit the bullseye some of the time (but not everytime). When it doesn't hit the bullseye, it's missing in all of the other buckets evenly (not just missing in the 16 bin) and it also misses closer to the bullseye as opposed to on the outer edges of the dartboard.

Coefficient of determination/R-squared–how well the model fits the data:

- The proportion of the variation explained by the model
- 1 is a perfect fit

The term error here represents the difference between the predicted value and the true value. The absolute value or the square of this difference are usually computed to capture the total magnitude of error across all instances, as the difference between the predicted and true values could be negative in some cases. The error metrics measure the predictive performance of a regression model in terms of the mean deviation of its predictions from the true values. Lower error values mean the model is more accurate in making predictions. An overall error metric of *0* means that the model fits the data perfectly.

We can then pass in a single feature vector to our trained model and it will return an expected label – you can view this part of the slide in two ways: the first is that it represents a single feature vector – for example, sepal width/length and petal width/length and our output will be the name of an iris plant or we can consider this as the leftover part of our data, usually 20% of it, which is then used to determine how effective our model is by guessing the labels that we already know from our trained model, which will allow us to find out whether we have a model that is good or bad.

The coefficient of determination, which is also known as R-squared, is also a standard way of measuring how well the model fits the data. It can be interpreted as the proportion of variation explained by the model. A higher proportion is better in this case, where 1 indicates a perfect fit.

Another measure that's useful for these continuous models is **Root Mean Square Deviation**, or **Root Mean Square Error** – in this case, we take the square root of the **MSE** – this will give us a perfect match to the scale of the Y-axis, so it will measure the average error rate in a scale that is a perfect measure of our prediction assessment.

Understanding the performance of the result

The p-value is an indicator that determines the result. It tests the theory that there was no difference in the results. In other words, it tests the null hypothesis that the coefficient is equal to zero, which means that, effectively, there is no difference between the items that you are testing.

A low p-value is usually denoted as < 0.05, or five percent. The p-value indicates that you can reject the null hypothesis. In other words, this means that the predictor is having an effect on the item that you are predicting, which is also known as the response variable.

A predictor that has a low p-value is likely to be a meaningful addition to your model. Changes in the predictor's value are related to changes in the item that you are predicting. If there was no relationship at all, then you would have a larger p-value. The large p-value would be said to be insignificant. This means that the predictor doesn't have a significant effect on the item that you are predicting.

Conversely, a larger (insignificant) p-value suggests that changes in the predictor are not associated with changes in the response.

With the first useful measure when we have a continuous model, for example, trying to predict a runners average pace in a race, which is a continuous not discrete, we will end up with a predicted pace or finish time that we can check against when the runner finishes the race.

In this case, we can sum up this and all of the other races that the runner has run and calculate the difference between all of the times we predicted and the actual times that the runner achieved. If we square this difference we get the **Mean Square Error**, which is a measure of how good our continuous model is–a zero **MSE** represents a perfect model where every prediction we made about the runner matches exactly what the runner achieved.

A great measure for the accuracy of our model is an extension of something that we looked at in the previous module when we considered correlation – we ended up with a correlation coefficient called R that gave us a measure between *-1* and *1*. R2 is generally used to show whether our continuous model is a good fit – it should yield a measure of *0* to *1* – *1* being a perfect fit.

The better the linear regression (on the right) fits the data in comparison to the simple average (on the left graph), the closer the value is to 1. The areas of the blue squares represent the squared residuals with respect to the continuous model. The areas of the red squares represent the squared residuals with respect to the average value (mean).

If we predict the iris classes we should be able to see that we got some of them right.

You can see here that out of 30 different types of iris data point measures we predicted 19 of them accurately – we need to consider these 19, but also the 11 we got wrong and how and why we got them wrong to understand the good parts and the bad parts of our model – the diagonal line in the center shows that we got 19 right.

This is somewhat harder to picture because this is a many class problem, but as long as each class boils down to state we can look at whether the model is viable for making predictions from the adult dataset.

Next steps

It is good governance to carry out continual evaluation of the data model. Ongoing testing and experimentation are essential for good business decisions, which are based on using machine learning. It may seem as if the analytical process is never finished. Why is this the case?

Andrew Grove wrote a book called *Only the Paranoid Survive*, which documented how Intel survived many changes and upsets in the computing industry throughout its history. Grove suggested that businesses are affected by six forces, both internal and external:

- Existing competition
- Complementary businesses
- Customers
- Potential customers
- Possibility of alternative ways of achieving the same end
- Suppliers

Grove proposed that if these forces stayed equivalent, that the company will steer a steady course. It's important to note that these forces are highly visible in terms of the data that the company receives. This data could come from websites, customer contacts, external competitive information, stock market APIs, and so on. Data changes over time and the internal and external forces can express themselves through these changes. This is why it's important to keep evaluating our models.

Within the CRISP-DM framework, evaluation is a key part of the process. It assesses the efficiency and validation of the model in preparation for deployment. It also lays out the steps required, and the instructions for carrying out those steps. It also includes a monitoring and maintenance plan, which summarizes the strategy for an ongoing review of the model's performance. It should detect any decline in model performance over time. Note that this is a cycle, and it is not a finished process. Once the models are put into production, they need to be continually checked against the data, and the original business question that they were supposed to answer. The model could be running in **Azure ML**, but its actual output and results may not be performing well against what it's actually intended to do.

With all machine learning, it's important to prove the model's worth over a series of results. It's important to look at the larger pattern of results, rather than simply any given specific result.

Sharing our data analysis using Tableau

R gives you good diagnostic information to help you take the next step in your analysis, which is to visualize the results.

Interpreting the results

Statistics provides us with a method of investigation where other methods haven't been able to help, and their success or failure isn't clear to many people. If we see a correlation and think that the relationship is obvious, then we need to think again. Correlation can help people to insinuate causation. It's often said that correlation is not causation, but what does this mean? Correlation is a measure of how closely related two things are. We can use other statistical methods, such as structural equation modeling, to help us to identify the direction of the relationship, if it exists, using correlated data. It's a complex field in itself, and it isn't covered in this book; the main point here is to show that this is a complex question.

How does correlation help us here? For our purposes, the most interesting statistic is the coefficient of determination, denoted $R2$ and pronounced R-squared, which indicates how well data points fit a statistical model –sometimes simply a line or curve. R-squared measures how close the data is to the fitted regression line. It is also known as the coefficient of multiple determination for multiple regression.

It can be explained by *R-squared = Explained variation/Total variation*, and it is always explained as a percentage between *0* and 100%: Generally speaking, the higher the R-squared value, then the better the model fits the data. In our example, our model fit is found to be 69%, which is reasonably successful. We would need to map out the data to visualize it better, and to see if the model fits a linear line or not.

Regression problems in business are trying to predict a continuous variable, such as the price of a car, or the amount of profit. In this example, we have created a model that can be used to predict sales. As a next step, we could try to pick apart the model to understand what variables are contributing to the success of the model, and which ones are not contributing.

Summary

In this chapter, we reviewed ways of creating regression models and displaying our regression results using Tableau. We have reiterated the importance of the business question in understanding the data, and we have covered interpretation of the statistics in terms of their numbers, whilst being mindful of the context.

While regression is important for scoring the data, there are business problems where we need to classify the data. Classification is one of the most important tasks in analytics today, and it's used in all sorts of examples to reach a business-oriented understanding of the business question.

5
Classifying Data with Tableau

In this chapter, we will look at ways to perform classification using R and visualizing the results in Tableau. Classification is one of the most important tasks in analytics today. By the end of this chapter, you'll build a decision tree, while retaining a focus on a business-oriented understanding of the business question using classification algorithms.

Business understanding

When we are modeling data, it is crucial to keep the original business objectives in mind. These business objectives will direct the subsequent work in the data understanding, preparation and modeling steps, and the final evaluation and selection (after revisiting earlier steps if necessary) of a classification model or models.

At later stages, this will help to streamline the project because we will be able to keep the model's performance in line with the original requirement, while retaining a focus on ensuring a return on investment from the project.

The main business objective is to identify individuals who are higher earners, so that they can be targeted by a marketing campaign. For this purpose, we will investigate the data mining of demographic data in order to create a classification model in R. The model will be able to accurately determine whether individuals earn a salary that is above or below $50K per annum. The datasets used in this chapter were taken from the **University of California Irvine Data** repository, which you can find at the following URL: https://archive.ics.uci.edu/ml/index.html. The dataset used is known as the Adult dataset, and it holds information on individuals such as age, level of education, sex, and current employment type.

The resulting model will be used to classify individuals for the marketing campaign. To do that, we must understand the predictive significance of each characteristic.

Understanding the data

We will use Tableau to look at data preparation and data quality. Though we could also do these activities in R, we will use Tableau since it is a good way of seeing data quality issues and capturing them easily. We can also see problematic issues such as outliers or missing values.

Data preparation

When confronted with many variables, analysts usually start by building a decision tree and then using the variables that the decision tree algorithm has selected with other methods that suffer from the complexity of many variables, such as neural networks. However, decision trees perform worse when the problem at hand is not linearly separable.

In this section, we will use Tableau as a visual data preparation in order to prepare the data for further analysis. Here is a summary of some of the things we will explore:

- Looking at columns that do not add any value to the model
- Columns that have so many missing categorical values that they do not predict the outcome reliably
- Review missing values from the columns

Describing the data

The dataset used in this project has 49,000 records. You can see from the files that the data has been divided into a training dataset and a test set. The training dataset contains approximately 32,000 records and the test dataset around 16,000 records.

It's helpful to note that there is a column that indicates the salary level or whether it is greater than or less than fifty thousand dollars per annum. This can be called a binomial label, which basically means that it can hold one or two possible values.

When we import the data, we can filter for records where no income is specified. There is one record that has a **NULL**, and we can exclude it. Here is the filter:

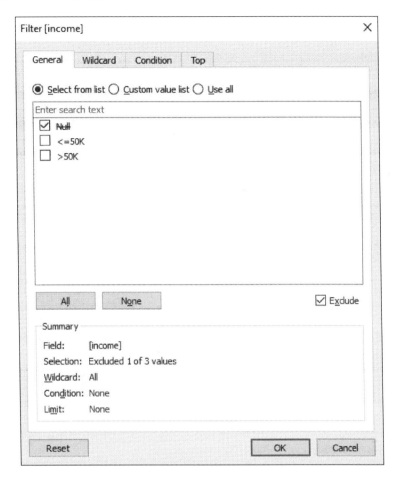

Let's explore the binomial label in more detail. How many records belong to each label?

Let's visualize the finding. Quickly, we can see that 76 percent of the records in the dataset have a class label of <50K.

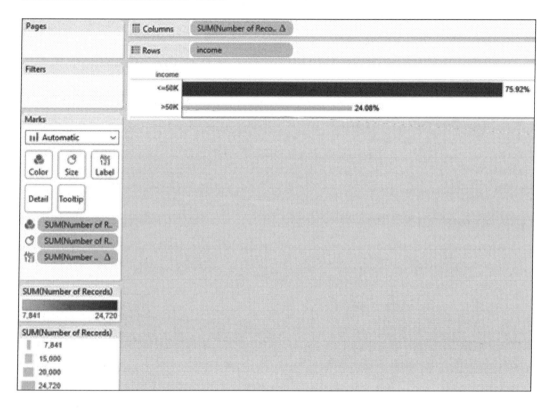

Let's have a browse of the data in Tableau in order to see what the data looks like. From the grid, it's easy to see that there are 14 attributes in total. We can see the characteristics of the data:

- **Seven polynomials:** workclass, education, marital-status, occupation, relationship, race, sex, native-country
- **One binomial:** sex
- **Six continuous attributes:** age, fnlwgt, education-num, capital-gain, capital-loss, hours-per-week

You can find out each individual value for each of the columns at the following website:

```
https://archive.ics.uci.edu/ml/machine-learning-databases/adult/
adult.names
```

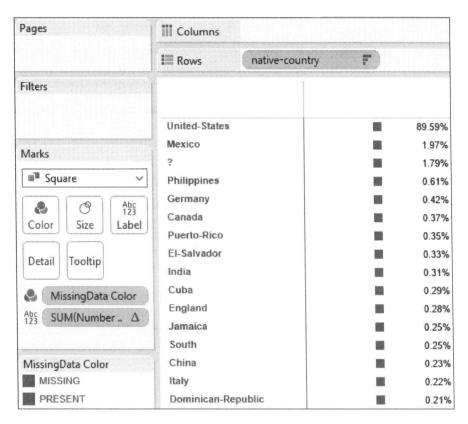

From the preceding chart, we can see that nearly 2 percent of the records are missing for one country, and the vast majority of individuals are from the United States. This means that we could consider the native-country feature as a candidate for removal from the model creation, because the lack of variation means that it isn't going to add anything interesting to the analysis.

Data exploration

We can now visualize the data in boxplots, so we can see the range of the data. In the first example, let's look at the age column, visualized as a boxplot in Tableau:

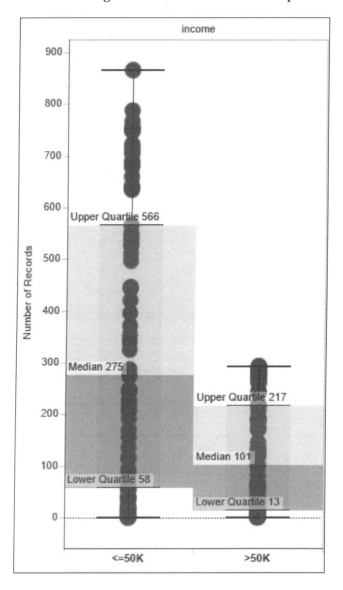

We can see that the values are higher for the age characteristic, and there is a different pattern for each income level.

When we look at education, we can also see a difference between the two groups:

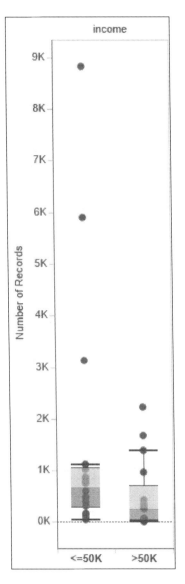

We can focus on age and education, while discarding other attributes that do not add value, such as native-country. The `fnlwgt` column does not add value because it is specific to the census collection process.

When we visualize the race feature, it's noted that the White value appears for 85 percent of overall cases. This means that it is not likely to add much value to the predictor:

race	
White	85.43%
Black	9.59%
Asian-Pac-Islander	3.19%
Amer-Indian-Eskimo	0.96%
Other	0.83%

Now, we can look at the number of years that people spend in education. When the education number attribute was plotted, then it can be seen that the lower values tend to predominate in the <50K class and the higher levels of time spent in education are higher in the >50K class. We can see this finding in the following figure:

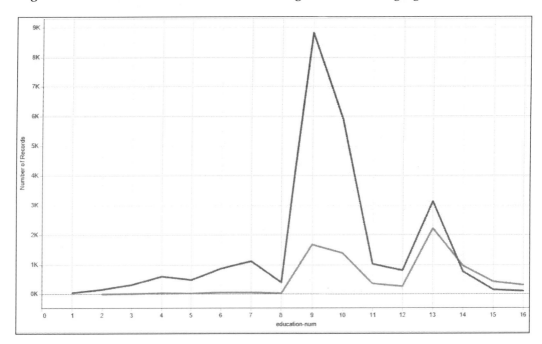

This finding may indicate some predictive capability in the education feature. The visualization suggests that there is a difference between both groups since the group that earns over $50K per annum does not appear much in the lower education levels. To summarize, we will focus on age and education as providing some predictive capability in determining the income level.

The purpose of the model is to classify people by their earning level. Now that we have visualized the data in Tableau, we can use this information in order to model and analyze the data in R to produce the model.

Modeling in R

In this example, we will use the `rpart` package, which is used to build a decision tree. The tree with the minimum prediction error is selected. After that, the tree is applied to make predictions for unlabeled data with the predict function.

One way to call `rpart` is to give it a list of variables and see what happens. Although we have discussed missing values, `rpart` has built-in code for dealing with missing values. So let's dive in, and look at the code.

Firstly, we need to call the libraries that we need:

```
library(rpart)
library(rpart.plot)
library(caret)
library(e1071)
library(arules)
```

Next, let's load in the data, which will be in the `AdultUCI` variable:

```
data("AdultUCI");

AdultUCI


## 75% of the sample size
sample_size <- floor(0.80 * nrow(AdultUCI))


## set the seed to make your partition reproductible
set.seed(123)


## Set a variable to have the sample size
```

```
training.indicator <- sample(seq_len(nrow(AdultUCI)), size = sample_size)


# Set up the training and test sets of data
adult.training <- AdultUCI[training.indicator, ]
adult.test <- AdultUCI[-training.indicator, ]


## set up the most important features
features <- AdultUCI$income ~ AdultUCI$age+AdultUCI$education+AdultUCI$"e
ducation-num"


# Let's use the training data to test the model
model<-rpart(features,data=adult.training)


# Now, let's use the test data to predict the model's efficiency
pred<-predict(model, adult.test ,type="class")


# Let's print the model
print(model)


# Results
#1) root 32561 7841 small (0.7591904 0.2408096)
#2) AdultUCI$"education-num"< 12.5 24494 3932 small (0.8394709 0.1605291)
*
#  3) AdultUCI$"education-num">=12.5 8067 3909 small (0.5154332
0.4845668)
#6) AdultUCI$age< 29.5 1617   232 small (0.8565244 0.1434756) *
#  7) AdultUCI$age>=29.5 6450 2773 large (0.4299225 0.5700775) *


printcp(model)

plotcp(model)
summary(model)
print(pred)
summary(pred)


# plot tree
```

```
plot(model, uniform=TRUE,
     main="Decision Tree for Adult data")
text(model, use.n=TRUE, all=TRUE, cex=.8)
```

```
prp(model, faclen = 0, cex = 0.5, extra = 1)
```

We can see the final result in the following diagram:

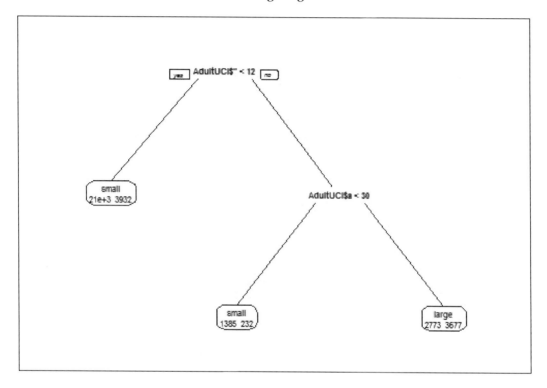

Analyzing the results of the decision tree

The decision tree grows from top to bottom. It starts with a root decision node. The branches from this node represent two—or possibly more—different options that are available to the decision makers.

At the end of the branches, we can find one of two things. Firstly, we may find an end node, which represents a fixed value. It can be understood as a stop in the decision process. Alternatively, we may find an uncertainty node, which has further possible outcomes available to it. If we were to add the probabilities of the uncertainty nodes together, they would sum to 1. Eventually, all of the branches will end in an end node.

Decision trees have inputs and outputs. In this example, we have provided the decision tree with a series of data. In R, they also output a number of data. Decision trees are useful because they provide easy model interpretation, and they also demonstrate the relevant importance of the variables.

Let's take a look at some of the main points of the results. From the output, we can see the following table, called `Variable importance`:

```
Variable importance
AdultUCI$"education-num"        AdultUCI$education
AdultUCI$age
44                      40                      16
```

This tells us that `education-num` has the highest percentage of importance, closely followed by education. Now, we could do some further analysis that would explore the correlation between these two items. If they are highly correlated, then we may consider removing one of them.

Next, we have the results for each of the nodes. In this section, we get the number of observations, probabilities, and the splits for each of the nodes, until the nodes reach an end.

Model deployment

Now that we have created our model, we can reuse it in Tableau. This model will just work in Tableau, as long as you have Rserve running. You will also need to have the relevant packages installed, as per the script. In particular, the `rpart` package is the workhorse of this example, and it must be installed since it is self-contained as it loads the library, trains the model, and then uses the model to make predictions within the same calculation.

There are many ways to deploy your model for future use, and this part of the process involves the CRISP-DM methodology. Here are a few ways:

- You can go through the model fitting inside R using RStudio or another IDE and save it. Then, you could simply load the model into Tableau or you can save it to a file directly from within Tableau. The advantage of doing it in this way is that you can reuse your R model in other packages as well. The downside is that you will need to switch between R and Tableau, and then back again.

- If you don't want to flip between R and Tableau, then you could add in an additional piece of code that would load the model directly from your location.

- You could also use the `eval` option. Eval executes the R code to follow. For example, if you had the following piece of code in your `Rserv.cfg` file, then it would load the model:

  ```
  eval load("C:/Users/bberan/R/mymodel.rda");
  ```

In this case, we see that the second line is loading the model we created. So the person who will use the model for predictions doesn't have to know where it is saved. If they know the name of the model, they can call it from Tableau. Note that the `config` file is read when Rserve starts, so if you made changes to the file you need to start Rserve for them to take effect. Also, by default Rserve looks for the `config` file in R's working directory. In R, you can find out what your working directory is using the `getwd()` command:

```
> getwd()
[1] "C:/Users/jenstirrup/Documents"
```

Then, we can start Rserve using the `Rserve()` command.

The `Rserv.cfg` file goes into the working directory. In this example, the working directory is at the following location: `C:/Users/jenst/Documents`. When Rserve is installed, it's possible for us to call the predict function from `rpart` directly from the code:

```
C:/Users/jenst/Documents
SCRIPT_REAL('mydata <- data.frame(admit=.arg1, gpa=.arg2, gre=.arg3,
rank=.arg4);
prob <- predict(lrmodel, newdata = mydata, type = "response")',
AVG([admit]),AVG([gpa]),AVG([gre]),AVG([rank]))
```

Decision trees in Tableau using R

When the data has a lot of features that interact in complicated non-linear ways, it is hard to find a global regression model, that is, a single predictive formula that holds over the entire dataset. An alternative approach is to partition the space into smaller regions, then into sub-partitions (recursive partitioning) until each chunk can be explained with a simple model.

There are two main types of decision trees:

- **Classification trees**: Predicted outcome is the class the data belongs to
- **Regression trees**: Predicted outcome is a continuous variable, for example, a real number such as the price of a commodity

There are many ensemble machine learning methods that take advantage of decision trees. Perhaps the best known is the **Random Forest** classifier that constructs multiple decision trees and outputs the class that corresponds to the mode of the classes output by individual trees.

Bayesian methods

Suppose I claim that I have a pair of magic rainbow socks. I allege that whenever I wear these special socks, I gain the ability to predict the outcome of coin tosses, using fair coins, better than chance would dictate. Putting my claim to the test, you toss a coin 30 times, and I correctly predict the outcome 20 times. Using a directional hypothesis with the binomial test, the null hypothesis would be rejected at alpha-level 0.05. Would you invest in my special socks?

Why not? If it's because you require a larger burden of proof on absurd claims, I don't blame you. As a grandparent of Bayesian analysis, *Pierre-Simon Laplace* (who independently discovered the theorem that bears *Thomas Bayes'* name), once said: The weight of evidence for an extraordinary claim must be proportioned to its strangeness. Our prior belief—my absurd hypothesis—is so small that it would take much stronger evidence to convince the skeptical investor, let alone the scientific community.

Unfortunately, if you'd like to easily incorporate your prior beliefs into NHST, you're out of luck. Or, suppose you need to assess the probability of the null hypothesis; you're out of luck there, too; NHST assumes the null hypothesis and can't make claims about the probability that a particular hypothesis is true. In cases like these (and in general), you may want to use Bayesian methods instead of frequentist methods. This section will tell you how. Join me!

The Bayesian interpretation of probability views probability as our degree of belief in a claim or hypothesis, and Bayesian inference tells us how to update that belief in the light of new evidence. In that chapter, we used Bayesian inference to determine the probability that employees of *Daisy Girl Inc.* were using an illegal drug. We saw how the incorporation of prior beliefs saved two employees from being falsely accused and helped another employee get the help she needed even though her drug screen was falsely negative.

In a general sense, Bayesian methods tell us how to dole out credibility to different hypotheses, given prior belief in those hypotheses and new evidence. In the drug example, the hypothesis suite was discrete: drug user or not drug user. More commonly, though, when we perform Bayesian analysis, our hypothesis concerns a continuous parameter, or many parameters. Our posterior (or updated beliefs) was also discrete in the drug example, but Bayesian analysis usually yields a continuous posterior called a posterior distribution.

We are going to use Bayesian analysis to put my magical rainbow socks claim to the test. Our parameter of interest is the proportion of coin tosses that I can correctly predict wearing the socks; we'll call this parameter θ, or *theta*. Our goal is to determine what the most likely values of theta are and whether they constitute proof of my claim.

The likelihood function is a binomial function, as it describes the behavior of Bernoulli trials; the binomial likelihood function for this evidence is shown in the following figure:

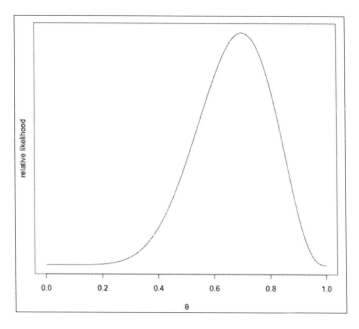

For different values of theta, there are varying relative likelihoods. Note that the value of theta that corresponds to the maximum of the likelihood function is 0.667, which is the proportion of successful Bernoulli trials. This means that in the absence of any other information, the most likely proportion of coin flips that my magic socks allow me to predict is 67 percent. This is called the **Maximum Likelihood Estimate (MLE)**.

So, we have the likelihood function; now we just need to choose a prior. We will be crafting a representation of our prior beliefs using a type of distribution called a beta distribution, for reasons that we'll see very soon.

Since our posterior is a blend of the prior and likelihood function, it is common for analysts to use a prior that doesn't much influence the results and allows the likelihood function to speak for itself. To this end, one may choose to use a non-informative prior that assigns equal credibility to all values of theta. This type of non-informative prior is called a flat or uniform prior.

The beta distribution has two hyper-parameters, a (or alpha) and β (or beta). A beta distribution with hyper-parameters $a = \beta = 1$ describes such a flat prior. We will call this *prior #1*:

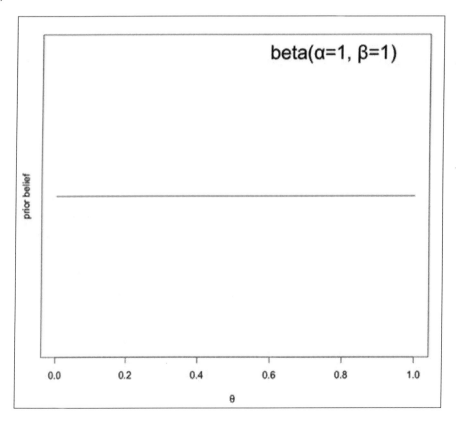

This prior isn't really indicative of our beliefs, is it? Do we really assign as much probability to my socks giving me perfect coin-flip prediction powers as we do to the hypothesis that I'm full of baloney?

The prior that a skeptic might choose in this situation is one that looks more like the one depicted in the next figure, a beta distribution with hyper-parameters *alpha* = *beta* = *50*. This, rather appropriately, assigns far more credibility to values of theta that are concordant with a universe without magical rainbow socks. As good scientists, though, we have to be open-minded to new possibilities, so this doesn't rule out the possibility that the socks give me special powers—the probability is low, but not zero, for extreme values of theta. We will call this *prior #2*:

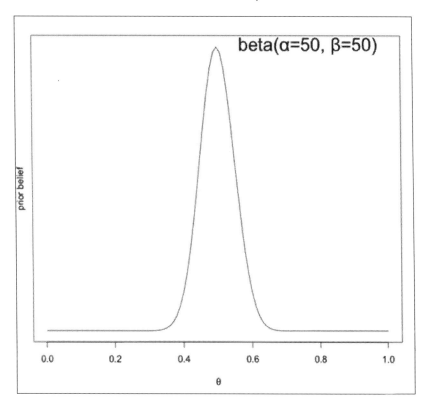

Before we perform the Bayesian update, I need to explain why I chose to use the beta distribution to describe my priors.

The Bayesian update—getting to the posterior—is performed by multiplying the prior with the likelihood. In the vast majority of applications of Bayesian analysis, we don't know what that posterior looks like, so we have to sample from it many times to get a sense of its shape. We will be doing this later in this chapter.

For cases like this, though, where the likelihood is a binomial function, using a beta distribution for our prior guarantees that our posterior will also be in the beta distribution family. This is because the beta distribution is a conjugate prior with respect to a binomial likelihood function. There are many other cases of distributions being self-conjugate with respect to certain likelihood functions, but it doesn't often happen in practice that we find ourselves in a position to use them as easily as we can for this problem. The beta distribution also has the nice property that it is naturally confined from *0* to *1*, just like the proportion of coin flips I can correctly predict.

The fact that we know how to compute the posterior from the prior and likelihood by just changing the beta distribution's hyper-parameters makes things really easy in this case. The hyper-parameters of the posterior distribution are:

$$new\,\alpha = old\,\alpha + number\ of\ successes$$
$$and$$
$$new\,\beta = old\,\beta + number\ of\ failures$$

That means the posterior distribution using *prior #1* will have hyper-parameters *alpha=1+20* and *beta=1+1*:

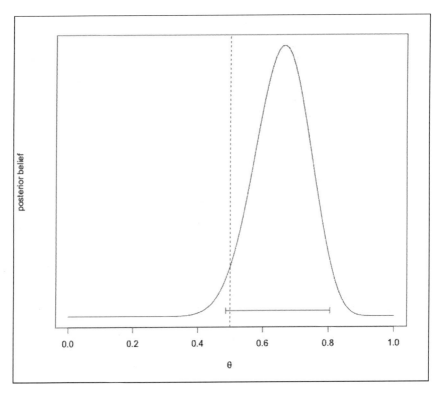

Do not confuse this with a confidence interval. Though it may look like it, this credible interval is very different than a confidence interval. Since the posterior directly contains information about the probability of our parameter of interest at different values, it is admissible to claim that there is a 95 percent chance that the correct parameter value is in the credible interval. We could make no such claim with confidence intervals. Please do not mix up the two meanings, or people will laugh you out of town.

Observe that the 95 percent most likely values for theta contain the theta value *0.5*, if only barely. Due to this, one may wish to say that the evidence does not rule out the possibility that I'm full of baloney regarding my magical rainbow socks, but the evidence was suggestive.

To be clear, the end result of our Bayesian analysis is the posterior distribution depicting the credibility of different values of our parameter. The decision to interpret this as sufficient or insufficient evidence for my outlandish claim is a decision that is separate from the Bayesian analysis proper. In contrast to NHST, the information we glean from Bayesian methods—the entire posterior distribution—is much richer. Another thing that makes Bayesian methods great is that you can make intuitive claims about the probability of hypotheses and parameter values in a way that frequentist NHST does not allow you to do.

What does that posterior using *prior #2* look like? It's a beta distribution with *alpha = 50+20* and *beta = 50+10*.

Graphs

A graph is a type of data structure capable of handling networks. Graphs are widely used across various domains such as the following:

- **Transportation**: To find the shortest routes to travel between two places
- **Communication-signaling networks**: To optimize the network of inter-connected computers and systems
- **Understanding relationships**: To build relationship trees across families or organizations
- **Hydrology**: To perform flow regime simulation analysis of various fluids

Terminology and representations

A graph (*G*) is a network of vertices (*V*) interconnected using a set of edges (*E*). Let | *V* | represent the count of vertices and | *E* | represent the count of edges. The value of | *E* | lies in the range of *0* to | *V* | *2* - | *V* |. Based on the directional edges, the graphs are classified as directed or undirected. In directed graphs, the edges are directed from one vertex towards the other, whereas in undirected graphs, each vertex has an equal probability of being directionally connected with the others. An undirected graph is said to be connected if all the vertices are connected with at least one edge. If the vertices are indexed, then it is said to be a labelled graph, and if the edges are associated with some value (cost or weights), then it is said to be a weighted graph. Adjacent vertices (*P* and *Q*) connected by an edge are termed as neighbors (*P*, *Q*), and the connecting edge is termed as an incident.

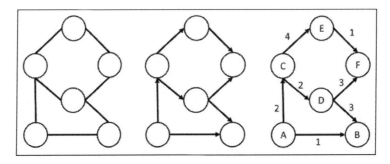

Consider a graph with n vertices. A sequence of interconnected vertices (*v1, v2, v3 ... vn*) is termed as a path, and the path is said to be simple if all the vertices of the path are unique. The length of the path is the number of edges, which is one less than the number of vertices (*n-1*). In case the vertices of a given path are not unique and the length of the path is greater than two, then the path becomes a cycle. A cycle is simple if all the intermediate vertices are unique and only the first and last vertices are the same. An undirected graph with no cycles is called an acyclic graph, and a directed graph with no cycles is called a **directed acyclic graph** (**DAG**).

Graph implementations

Let us create an **Abstract Data Type** (**ADT**) — (Graph_ADT) for the implementation of functions on a given graph. The key features of ADT for a given graph analysis are the following:

- Fixed number of vertices
- Provision for addition and deletion of edges
- Provision to support a mark array, which can assist algorithms in traversing along the graph

The vertices are denoted using non-zero integer values, and can additionally store vertex names or some kinds of application-based predetermined values. The following are some ADT functions that are widely used for implementing graph functions:

- `num_vert`: This function returns the number of vertices for a given graph.

- `num_edge`: This function returns the number of edges for a given graph.

- `weightEdge`: This function returns the weight of an edge connecting two adjacent vertices. Its input is a pair of two connected vertices and its output is a numeric value indicating its weight.

- `assignEdge`: This function is used to assign weight to a given edge of a graph. The input is a pair of vertices. It can take in only a non-zero positive value, as a zero value means no connection (thereby no assignment required) and a negative value can skew the computational results.

- `deleteEdge`: This function is used to delete the weight of a given edge. The input is a pair of vertices, which has a connected edge.

- `firstVertex`: This function returns the index of the first edge vertex based on a sorted list of vertices, which are connected to a given vertex. The input is a vertex for a given graph.

- `nextVertex`: This function returns the subsequent index of vertices for a given pair of connected vertices such that the returned vertex will have an edge connecting to the first vertex. Assume that *V1* is connected with *V2* and *V3* such that the index values of *V2* are less than *V3*. Then, the `firstVertex` function will return the edge vertex of *V1* as *V2* (as the index value of *V2* is less than *V3*), and the `nextVertex` function will return *V3*, as it is a subsequent connected vertex index of *V1* for a given *V2*.

- `isEdge`: This function returns a Boolean number, where *1* represents the presence of an edge, and *0* represents the absence of an edge.

- `getMark`: This function returns the mark of a given vertex from an array mark.

- `initMark`: This function marks the unmarked vertex in an array mark.

Summary

Although most introductory data analysis texts don't even broach the topic of Bayesian methods, you, dear reader, are versed enough in this matter to start applying these techniques to real problems.

We discovered that Bayesian methods could—at least for the models in this chapter—not only allow us to answer the same kinds of questions we might use the binomial, one sample t-test, and the independent samples t-test for, but provide a much richer and more intuitive depiction of our uncertainty in our estimates. If these approaches interest you, I urge you to learn more about how to extend these to supersede other NHST tests. I also urge you to learn more about the mathematics behind MCMC. As with the last chapter, we covered much ground here. If you made it through, congratulations! This concludes the unit on confirmatory data analysis and inferential statistics. In the next unit, we will be less concerned with estimating parameters, and more interested in prediction. Last one there is a rotten egg!

This current chapter covered the fundamentals of graphs and introduced terminology and representation. The later sections of this chapter covered searching techniques in graphs using **DFS** and **BFS**. This chapter also introduced in-order search in scenarios where nodes are conditionally dependent. The chapter also covered the **Dijkstra** algorithm widely used to estimate single-source shortest paths regardless of their directions. The concept of MST was introduced with algorithms such as **Prim** and **Kruskal**, which were covered to extract MST from a directed and weighted graph. The next chapter will extend coverage of static algorithms to randomized algorithms, and will also introduce the fundamentals of programming.

6
Advanced Analytics Using Clustering

Wouldn't it be great if you could analyze your customers better, by classifying them into groups? Or perhaps even look at crime types in groups? Do you have problems with grouping large amounts of data in a meaningful way? On the flip side, do you have problems in distinguishing groups of data?

Data often has groups hidden in it. For example, we can group people by income, education, age, or where they live. We could also group people by their values, community involvements, family members, school membership, and other personal characteristics. We can find all sorts of insights by grouping our data together.

Tableau brings you good news! The clustering process just got much easier in Tableau 10. Tableau has a brand new clustering feature, which groups similar data points together. Tableau makes it easy for you to find interesting patterns in data. Even better, Tableau offers a full clustering experience on any type of visualization that you want to use, and that even includes maps!

Tableau makes it easy to solve very practical business problems that can be addressed by clustering. In this chapter, we will look at using clustering techniques in both R and in Tableau, in order to solve these common business issues.

What is Clustering?

Here we represent the elbow curve and the best number of clusters on it, which are represented on the curve line:

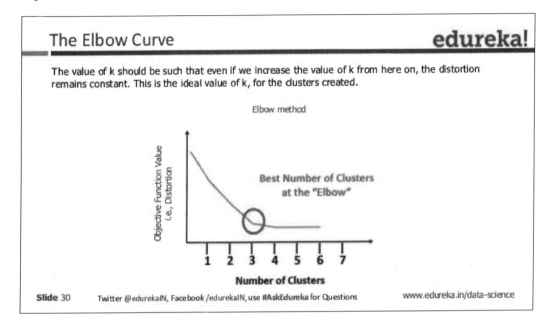

Clustering is a way of analyzing data so that the items are grouped into similar groups, or clusters, according to their similarity. Clustering is the process of finding interesting patterns in data, and it is used to categorize and classify data into groups, as well as to distinguish groups of data from each other. Before we start to cluster the data, we don't know the cluster where each data point resides.

Clustering is an example of an unsupervised method. In unsupervised methods of machine learning, unsupervised methods are not focused on trying to predict an outcome. Instead, unsupervised methods are focused on discovering patterns in the data. Using unsupervised methods means that you can take a fresh look at the data for patterns that you may not have considered previously, such as neural networks or clustering, for example.

Clustering is a great tool for exploring data and reducing complexities, so it can help you to analyze data, particularly where there are no obvious distinctions contained in the data.

Now, clustering is an essential tool in the analytics toolkit. Tableau reduces the learning friction by including it as a key part of the user interface. We will look at the clustering features in Tableau in the first part of this chapter. Then, we will look at the facilities for clustering in R. The purpose is not to compare Tableau versus R. Instead, we are exploring the opportunities for using both tools for advanced analytics.

The key to success in implementing clustering models is to create a new model that will make its predictions based solely on previous rewards and punishments for similar predictions made on similar datasets.

Finding clusters in data

Cluster analysis partitions marks in the view into clusters, where the marks within each cluster are more similar to one another than they are to marks in other clusters.

In Tableau Desktop, you create clusters by dragging **Cluster** from the **Analytics** pane and dropping it in the view. Now you will see that there is a statistical object. Here, Tableau places it on the **Color** shelf. Note that, if there is already a field on Color, Tableau moves that field to Detail and replaces it on Color with the clustering results.

Using clustering, Tableau assigns each mark to one of the clusters on the canvas. If any of the marks do not fit well in one of the clusters, then it is put into a not clustered cluster.

Clustering has its own dialog box, which allows you to add a cluster, or edit a cluster that exists already. The clustering dialog box gives you a lot of flexibility and control over the clustering process, whilst also giving you the ability to use suggested features. For example, you can indicate the number of clusters, or stay with Tableau's proposed number of clusters.

Tableau offers the dialogue box to enable the exploration process too. Tableau uses variables in order to compute clusters, and the dialog allows you to add variables or take them away so you can explore the data visually and easily. You can change the aggregations too, which will further allow you to explore interesting nuances in the data.

Let's drag a **Cluster** over to the **Data** pane. You will see that it becomes a group dimension, with the clusters appearing as individual members of the dimension. Each cluster contains the individual marks that are classified as being part of each cluster.

Your analysis can flow easily from worksheet to worksheet, as your cluster isn't restricted to the current worksheet.

For more details you can refer to *Create a Tableau Group from Cluster Results* article found at: `http://onlinehelp.tableau.com/v10.0/pro/desktop/en-us/clustering_group.html`.

Why can't I drag my Clusters to the Analytics pane?

Sometimes, you might find that you can't drag your clusters over to the canvas. Why is that? Well, unfortunately, clustering isn't available in every scenario. Throughout this book, we have been using clustering on the Tableau Desktop, but, unfortunately, clustering is not available for authoring on the web.

Clustering is also not available for every single data source. So, for example, it's not possible to use clustering if you are using a multidimensional cube source, or if you have a blended dimension. Furthermore, certain Tableau constructs can't be used as inputs for clustering. These include certain types of calculations such as table calculations, blended calculations, or ad-hoc calculations. Other Tableau constructs that can't be used as variables include groups, sets, bins, or parameters.

To summarize, it isn't possible to use every Tableau construct. That being said, clustering can also surprise you with its insights, and there are still plenty of features to explore.

Clustering in Tableau

Tableau's power has always been its user-focused flexibility, and working with the user in order to achieve insights at the speed of thought. Tableau's clustering functionality continues the tradition of putting the user front-and-center of the analytics process. So, for example, Tableau allows us to quickly customize geographical areas, for example, which in turn can yield new insights and patterns held within the groups.

Tableau 10.0 comes with **k-means** clustering as a built-in function. K-means is a popular clustering algorithm that is useful, easy to implement, and it can be faster than some other clustering methods, particularly in the case of big datasets.

We can see the data being grouped, or clustered, around centers. The algorithm works firstly by choosing the cluster centers randomly. Then, it works out the nearest cluster centers, and arranges the data points around it.

K-means then works out the actual cluster center. It then reassigns the data points to the new cluster center. These steps are repeated until the data. The filled shapes represent the center of the cluster.

How does k-means work?

K-means procedure splits the data into K segments. Each segment has a centroid that corresponds to the average value for the marks in that segment. The objective of the k-means procedure is to place the centroids so that the total of the sum of distances between centroids and marks in respective segments is as small as possible.

How to do Clustering in Tableau

In order to create clustering in tableau we need to follow the next:

- In Tableau, go to the **Analytics** pane on the left-hand side
- Drag **Cluster** from the **Analytics** pane onto the current canvas view

You can explore your data by dragging the cluster in and out of the pane so that you can compare.

Clustering feature has a describe dialog that gives you summary statistics for each cluster to help you to understand how Tableau has obtained the results with the clustering process.

Creating Clusters

To find clusters in a view in Tableau, follow these steps:

1. Create a view.

2. Drag **Cluster** from the **Analytics** pane into the view, and drop it on the target area in the view:

   You can also double-click **Cluster** to find clusters in the view.

   Two things happen when you drop or double-click **Cluster**:

   ◦ Tableau adds Clusters on **Color**, and colors the marks in your view by cluster

○ Tableau displays a **Clusters** dialog box, where you can customize the cluster:

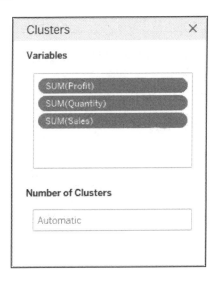

3. Customize the cluster results by doing either of the following in the Clusters dialog box:

   ○ Drag new fields from the **Data** pane into the **Variables** area of the **Clusters** dialog box

   When you add variables, measures are aggregated using the default aggregation for the field; dimensions are aggregated using ATTR, which is the standard way that Tableau aggregates dimensions.

   ○ Specify the number of clusters. If you do not specify a value, Tableau will go as high as 25 clusters in trying to determine the number of clusters. If you specify a value, you can choose any number between 2 and 50.

4. When you finish customizing the cluster results, click the **X** in the upper-right corner of the **Clusters** dialog box to close it:

You can move the cluster field from **Color** to another shelf in the view. However, you cannot move the cluster field from the Filters shelf to the **Data** pane.

To edit **Clusters** you have previously created, right-click (Control-click on a Mac) the **Clusters** field on **Color** and choose **Edit** clusters.

Or for an example showing the process of creating clusters with sample data (world economic indicators), see *Example - Create Clusters from World Economic Indicators Data* here: http://onlinehelp.tableau.com/v10.0/pro/desktop/en-us/clustering_example.html.

If you aren't sure how many splits to use, there's no need to worry! As you know, Tableau already makes things very easy for you, by proposing the correct data visualization for you. Well, Tableau also makes analytics easier for you, by recommending the number of splits that you need. This is particularly helpful if you are simply exploring the data.

Tableau is flexible, and it offers you the ability to specify your own clustering settings. For example, you can stipulate the number of clusters that you would like to create. This is a process that is similar to creating bins in Tableau. Bins have to be an equal size, however clustering allows you the flexibility to have varying sizes of clusters. This may be the preferred option if you have business reasons for wanting to combine things a little differently, and Tableau has the flexibility of allowing you to specify the number of clusters, or finding that information for you.

Once you identify the clusters, you can assign them more intuitive names based on the summaries for each cluster (which, in this case, can be seen in the scatter plots). In this example, we have three clusters corresponding to developed, developing, and underdeveloped countries based on the four metrics used as the clustering criteria.

You can use clustering results in other visualizations such as dimensions. You can even manually override cluster assignments if you have external domain knowledge that you want to incorporate into the results.

Clustering example in Tableau

In the example, we are going to use clustering to drag the cluster pill from the sheet into the data pane on the left. You can treat the resulting field as a group. In your visualizations, Tableau will treat the cluster field like any other visualization.

These include standardization of inputs that automatically scale the data and multiple correspondence analyses (if you're curious about the details, you can find out more about the math behind clustering in product documentation at `http://onlinehelp.tableau.com/v10.0/pro/desktop/en-us/help.html#clustering.html`).

This means you can work with many different types of data with minimal preparation. You can include categorical fields such as `education level` in your clustering analysis alongside numeric variables such as `income` without worries or use it for clustering survey responses where all inputs could be categorical.

Creating a Tableau group from cluster results

Drag **Clusters** from the **Marks** card (or from any other shelf you had already dragged it to) to the **Data** pane to create a Tableau group:

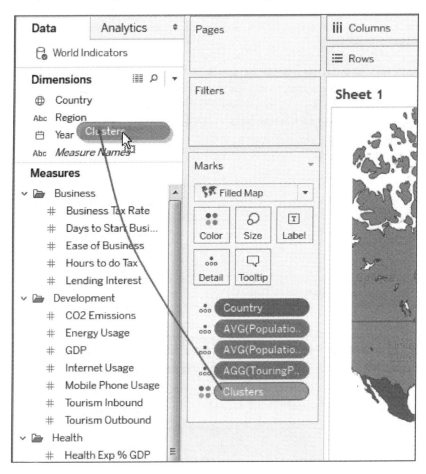

After you create a group from clusters, the group and the original clusters are separate and distinct. Editing the clusters does not affect the group, and editing the group does not affect the cluster results. The group has the same characteristics as any other Tableau group. It is part of the data source. Unlike the original clusters, you can use the group in other worksheets in the workbook. So if you rename the saved cluster group, that renaming is not applied to the original clustering in the view. You can get more information about Groups at `http://onlinehelp.tableau.com/v10.0/pro/desktop/en-us/sortgroup_groups.html`.

Constraints on saving Clusters

You will not be able to save **Clusters** to the **Data** pane under any of the following circumstances:

- When the measures in the view are disaggregated and the measures you are using as clustering variables are not the same as the measures in the view. You can get more information about disaggregating data at `http://onlinehelp.tableau.com/v10.0/pro/desktop/en-us/calculations_aggregation_disaggregatingdata.html`.

- When the Clusters you want to save are on the **Filters** shelf.

- When `Measure Names` or `Measure Values` is in the view.

- When there is a blended dimension in the view.

If you're looking for clusters in your sheet, just drag **Cluster** from the Analytics pane into the view. To see how different inputs change clustering results, you can experiment by dragging them in and out of the dialog and seeing the results in real time.

Interpreting your results

Sometimes groupings in data make immediate sense. When clustering by income and age, one could come across a group that can be labeled as `young professionals`.

In UN development indicators dataset, using the **Describe** dialog, one can clearly see that `Cluster 1`, `Cluster 2`, and `Cluster 3` correspond to `Underdeveloped`, `Developing`, and `Highly Developed` countries, respectively. By doing so we're using k-means to compress the information that is contained in three columns and 180+ rows to just three labels. Clustering can sometimes also find patterns your dataset may not be able to sufficiently explain by itself.

For example, as you're clustering health records, you may find two distinct groups and why? is not immediately clear and describable with the available data, which may lead you to ask more questions and maybe later realize that difference was because one group exercised regularly while the other didn't, or one had an immunity to a certain disease. It may even indicate things such as fraudulent activity/drug abuse, which otherwise you may not have noticed. Given it is hard to anticipate and collect all relevant data, such hidden patterns are not uncommon in real life.

How Clustering Works in Tableau

Cluster analysis partitions the marks in the view into clusters, where the marks within each cluster are more similar to one another than they are to marks in other clusters. Tableau distinguishes clusters using color.

For additional insight into how clustering works in Tableau, see the blog post *Understanding Clustering in Tableau 10* at `https://boraberan.wordpress.com/2016/07/19/understanding-clustering-in-tableau-10/`.

The clustering algorithm

Tableau uses the k-means algorithm for clustering. For a given number of clusters k, the algorithm partitions the data into k clusters. Each cluster has a center (centroid) that is the mean value of all the points in that cluster. The k-means locates centers through an iterative procedure that minimizes distances between individual points in a cluster and the cluster center. In Tableau, you can specify a desired number of clusters, or have Tableau test different values of k and suggest an optimal number of clusters (see *Determining the optimal number of clusters* section at `http://onlinehelp.tableau.com/v10.0/pro/desktop/en-us/clustering_howitworks.html#Determining_the_Optimal_Number_of_Clusters` for further details).

K-means requires an initial specification of cluster centers. Starting with one cluster, the method chooses a variable whose mean is used as a threshold for splitting the data in two. The centroids of these two parts are then used to initialize k-means to optimize the membership of the two clusters. Next, one of the two clusters is chosen for splitting and a variable within that cluster is chosen whose mean is used as a threshold for splitting that cluster in two. K-means is then used to partition the data into three clusters, initialized with the centroids of the two parts of the split cluster and the centroid of the remaining cluster. This process is repeated until a set number of clusters is reached.

Tableau uses the **Lloyd** algorithm with squared Euclidean distances to compute the k-means clustering for each k. Combined with the splitting procedure to determine the initial centers for each $k > 1$, the resulting clustering is deterministic, with the result dependent only on the number of clusters.

Scaling

Tableau scales values automatically so that columns having a larger range of magnitudes don't dominate the results. For example, an analyst could be using inflation and GDP as input variables for clustering, but because GDP values are in trillions of dollars, this could cause the inflation values to be almost completely disregarded in the computation. Tableau uses a scaling method called min-max normalization, in which the values of each variable are mapped to a value between *0* and *1* by subtracting its minimum and dividing by its range.

Clustering without using k-means

Now, Tableau can only do k-Means clustering. On the other hand, R can offer a variety of other clustering methodologies, such as hierarchical clustering.

In this topic, we will look at how R can do other types of clustering, which completes the picture of clustering in Tableau.

Hierarchical modeling

Hierarchical modeling is aimed at finding hierarchies of clusters. This facility is available to us in R. To do this, let's use the `Iris` dataset with an R script, which will focus on hierarchical clustering. The script is as follows:

```
IrisSample <- sample(1:dim(iris)[1],40)
IrisSample$Species <- NULL

dim(IrisSample)
hc <- hclust(dist(IrisSample), method="ave")
hc

plot(hc, hang = -1, labels=iris$Species[IrisSample])
```

In the following figure we can represent a cluster dendogram, which means the hierarchies of clusters.

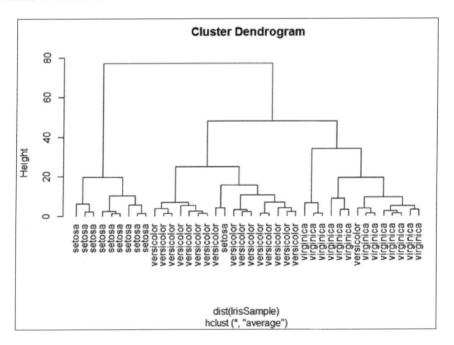

Statistics for Clustering

The **Describe Clusters** dialog box provides information about the models that Tableau computed for clustering. You can use these statistics to assess the quality of the clustering.

When the view includes clustering, you can open the **Describe Clusters** dialog box by right-clicking **Clusters** on the **Marks** card (Control-clicking on a Mac) and choosing **Describe Clusters**. The information in the **Describe Clusters** dialog box is read-only, though you can click **Copy to Clipboard** and then paste the screen contents into a writeable document.

The **Describe Clusters** dialog box has two tabs: a **Summary** tab and a **Models** tab.

Describing Clusters – Summary tab

These are described in the following table:

Number of Clusters	The number of individual clusters in the clustering.
Number of Points	The number of marks in the view.
Between-group sum of squares	A metric quantifying the separation between clusters as a sum of squared distances between each cluster's centre (average value), weighted by the number of data points assigned to the cluster, and the centre of the data set. The larger the value, the better the separation between clusters.
Within-group sum of squares	A metric quantifying the cohesion of clusters as a sum of squared distances between the centre of each cluster and the individual marks in the cluster. The smaller the value, the more cohesive the clusters.
Total sum of squares	Totals the between-group sum of squares and the within-group sum of squares. The ratio (between-group sum of squares)/(total sum of squares) gives the proportion of variance explained by the model.
Cluster Statistics	For each cluster in the clustering, the following information is provided.
# Items	The number of marks within the cluster.
Centers	The average value within each cluster (shown for numeric items).
Most Common	The most common value within each cluster (only shown for categorical items).

Testing your Clustering

Since clustering models are unsupervised, they can be harder to evaluate. The clusters are created by the modeling procedure, and it's not immediately obvious how the clusters were generated.

Evaluation is a matter of checking observable summaries about the clustering. There are some key metrics that need to be taken into consideration, and they are discussed next.

Describing Clusters – Models Tab

Analysis of variance (ANOVA) is a collection of statistical models and associated procedures useful for analyzing variation within and between observations that have been partitioned into groups or clusters. In this case, analysis of variance is computed per variable, and the resulting analysis of variance table can be used to determine which variables are most effective for distinguishing clusters.

Relevant Analysis of variance statistics for Tableau clustering include:

- **F-statistic**: The F-statistic for one-way, or single-factor, ANOVA is the fraction of variance explained by a variable. It is the ratio of the between-group variance to the total variance.

   The larger the F-statistic, the better the corresponding variable is distinguishing between clusters.

- **p-value**: The p-value is the probability that the F-distribution of all possible values of the F-statistic takes on a value greater than the actual F-statistic for a variable. If the p-value falls below a specified significance level, then the null hypothesis (that the individual elements of the variable are random samples from a single population) can be rejected. The degrees of freedom for this F- distribution are $(k - 1, N - k)$, where k is the number of clusters and N is the number of items (rows) clustered.

   The lower the p-value, the more the expected values of the elements of the corresponding variable differ among clusters.

- **Model Sum of Squares and degrees of freedom**: The Model Sum of Squares is the ratio of the between-group sum of squares to the model degrees of freedom. The between group sum of squares is a measure of the variation between cluster means. If the cluster means are close to each other (and therefore close to the overall mean), this value will be small. The model has k-1 degrees of freedom, where *k* is the number of clusters.

- **Error Sum of Squares** and **Degrees of Freedom**: The Error Sum of Squares is the ratio of within-group sum of squares to the error degrees of freedom. The within-group sum-of-squares measures the variation between observations within each cluster. The error has *N-k* degrees of freedom, where *N* is the total number of observations (rows) clustered and k is the number of clusters.

  The Error Sum of Squares can be thought of as the overall Mean Square Error, assuming that each cluster center represents the "truth" for each cluster.

Introduction to R

The R language, as the descendant of the statistics language, **S**, has become the preferred computing language in the field of statistics. Moreover, due to its status as an active contributor in the field, if a new statistical method is discovered, it is very likely that this method will first be implemented in the R language. As such, a large quantity of statistical methods can be fulfilled by applying the R language.

To apply statistical methods in R, the user can categorize the method of implementation into descriptive statistics and inferential statistics:

- **Descriptive statistics**: These are used to summarize the characteristics of the data. The user can use mean and standard deviation to describe numerical data, and use frequency and percentages to describe categorical data.

- **Inferential statistics**: Based on the pattern within sample data, the user can infer the characteristics of the population. The methods related to inferential statistics are for hypothesis testing, data estimation, data correlation, and relationship modeling. Inference can be further extended to forecasting, prediction, and estimation of unobserved values either in or associated with the population being studied.

Summary

Our goal was to deliver clustering examples with results that are repeatable with good performance. This is a tough balancing act, and it's important to keep. Quality and repeatability are must haves for trusting the results while good performance encourages experimentation with different filters, levels of detail, input variables, and so on, which is the path to more insights.

In the next chapter we will see how to an unsupervised learning technique requires a different approach than the ones you have seen previously.

7

Advanced Analytics with Unsupervised Learning

Would you like to know how to make predictions from a dataset? Alternatively, would you like to find exceptions, or outliers that you need to watch out for?

Neural networks are used in business to answer these business questions. They are used to make predictions from a dataset, or to find unusual patterns. They are best used for regression or classification business problems.

In this chapter, we will look at neural networks as a specific example of advanced analytics, and how they can be used to answer real-life business questions.

What are neural networks?

Neural networks are one of the most interesting machine learning models. Neural networks are inspired by the structures of the brain. Neural networks are algorithms that mimic the functioning of the brain. They are unsupervised algorithms, which means that we do not always know what the outputs should be.

Neural networks have layers, which can be categorized into the following:

- Input
- Middle
- Output layers

The input layer consumes the data, and the output layer represents the result. The middle layer represents the part of the algorithm that indicates how the input layer gets to the output layer.

Different types of neural networks

The simplest type of neural network is known as a **Feedforward Neural Network**. It feeds information in one direction only, from the front to the back. This type of network is also known as a perceptron. The following figure illustrates a perceptron:

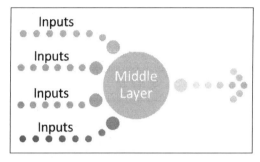

Neural network training process

Neural networks can also feed information back down through the layers. One method for this process is known as **backpropagation**, which feeds back through the system to generate the difference between the target and actual output values.

 Neural nets are complex because they contain many hidden layers. The middle layer works to map the inputs to the outputs. To achieve this function, the neural network needs to undergo a lot of training.

Here is an illustration of how these neural networks might look. Error is fed back to modify future learning iteration:

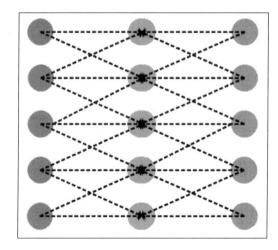

Training involves getting the errors from the first pass through the learning process. The error is then fed back through the network, and it's used to help point the neural network more closely to the expected output.

At its most basic level, the neural network consumes a number of inputs, and tries to crunch the data down to a small number of outputs. The inputs are made up of the values in a data record, and the output layer is represented by a node, which could be 1 for correct, and 0 for the others.

The neural network does this by creating a middle layer, which looks at various ways in which the numbers can be manipulated and combined to produce results that are as close to the target as possible.

The number of layers and the processing points within the layer are part of the black magic of the data scientist. Sometimes this is a best fit, and sometimes it isn't a black and white, clear cut answer. There are several guidelines, however, that might help in the process.

Firstly, as the complexity in the input and output increases, then the number of processing points in the hidden layer will also increase. Furthermore, if the model can be split out into separate stages, then different layers may be incorporated into the model.

Backpropagation and Feedforward neural networks

Training a neural network is an iterative process, which involves discovering values for its weights and its bias terms. These are used in conjunction with the input values to create outputs. After much iteration, the model is tested for the purposes of becoming a full production model that can be used to make predictions.

Training a neural network model is an iterative process, which is a key part of the **Cross Industry Standard Process** for **Data Mining (CRISP-DM)** as an integral part of the modeling phase. Training involves working out weights and bias values that lead the inputs towards the preferred output. As part of the training process, the model can be presented with the test data in order to evaluate its accuracy. This will help us to understand how well the model will perform when it is given new data, and we don't know the true output results.

During the training process, rows are presented to the neural network consecutively, one at a time. The weights associated with each input value are adjusted each time. Then, once all the rows from the training set are presented, the process starts again. During the model learning phase, the neural network adjusts the weights so that the cases are predicted by the correct output nodes.

The weights and functions in the hidden layer are readjusted so that the resulting findings are compared against the actual outputs. The error value is then fed back through the system, hence the name backpropagation. The middle layer is then adjusted to cater for the next inbound record.

It should be noted that the same training set of data can be processed many times throughout the training process. Once this is deemed to be completed, the test data is presented to the network to see how well it performs.

Finally, it's crucial to split your data into training and test data. The training data sets an upper bound for the number of processing points in the hidden layer.

It would be strange, for example, if the number of points was greater than the number of training cases. It's possible to calculate the upper bound by using the number of training cases, and divide it by sum of the number of nodes in both the input and output layers in the network. Then, we take that result and divide it by a scaling factor between five and ten. If the data is less noisy, then it's possible to use a larger scaling factor. This process can help us to get a balance between training individual cases, and making the network inefficient to deal with new datasets.

Evaluating a neural network model

Another fundamental phase of the CRISP-DM methodology is the evaluation phase, which focuses on the quality of the model, and its ability to meet the overall business objectives. If the model can't meet the objectives, then it's important to understand if there is a business reason why the model doesn't meet the objectives, in addition to technical possibilities that might account for failure. It's also a good time to pause and consider the testing results that you have generated thus far. This is a crucial stage because it can reveal challenges that didn't appear before. That said, it is an interesting phase because you can find new and interesting things for future research directions. Therefore, it's important not to skip it!

Fortunately, we can visualize the results using Tableau so that the neural networks are easier to understand. There are several performance measures for neural networks, and we will explore these in more detail along with a discussion of how the performance measures are visualized. You can view the results as **Receiver Operator Characteristic (ROC)** curves, **Precision/Recall** curves, or **Lift** curves. Additional data visualizations could include a confusion matrix, and cumulative values for the area under the curve (AUC). Let's look at these measurements in more detail.

Neural network performance measures

In the meantime, however, let's make the concepts of the neural net clear by looking at the options for visualizing the results.

Receiver Operating Characteristic curve

Here is an example of a **Receiver Operator Characteristic (ROC)** curve, where we can see the data analysis and the changes we have in the data accordingly to the time.

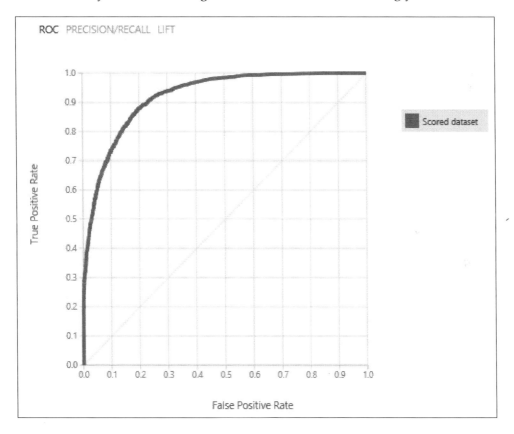

The closer this curve is to the upper left corner, the better the model's performance is. It means it is better at identifying the true positive rate while minimizing the false positive rate. In this example, we can see that the model is performing well.

Precision and Recall curve

Precision and Recall curve are very useful for assessing models in terms of business questions. They offer more detail and insights into the model's performance. Here is an example:

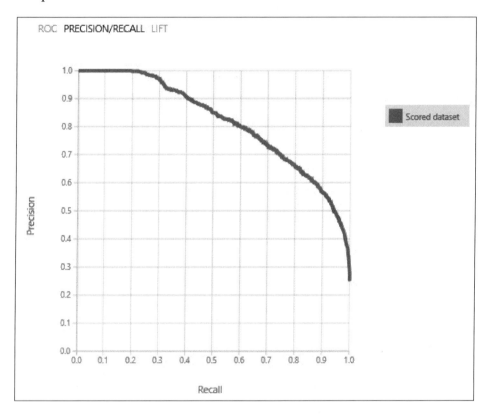

Precision can be described as the fraction of times that the model classifies the number of cases correctly. It can be considered as a measure of confirmation, and it indicates how often the model is correct.

Recall is a measure of utility, which means that it identifies how much the model finds of all that there is to find within the search space. Both scores combine to make the F1 score. The F1 score combines Precision and Recall. If either precision or recall is small, then the F1 score value will be small.

Lift scores

We can also look at the lift score. A lift chart visually represents the improvement that a model provides when compared against a random guess. Here is an example lift chart in the following screenshot:

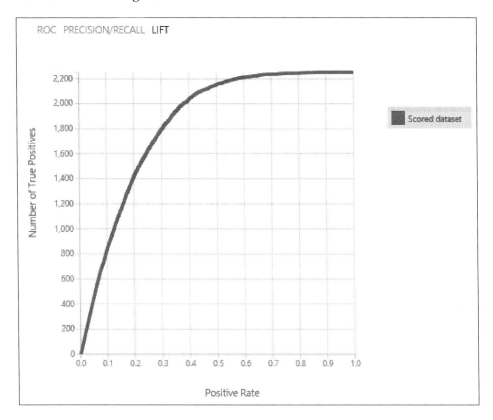

This is called a lift score. With a lift chart, you can compare the accuracy of predictions for the models that have the same predictable attribute.

Visualizing neural network results

Let's work through an example of a neural network, using publicly accessible data. We will use R to create the neural network, and then we will visualize the results in Tableau.

Neural network in R

Let's load up the libraries that we need. We are going to use the `neuralnet` package. The `neuralnet` package is a flexible package that is created for the training of neural networks using the backpropagation method. We discussed the backpropagation method previously in this chapter.

Let's install the package using the following command:

```
install.packages("neuralnet")
```

Now, let's load the library:

```
library(neuralnet)
```

We need to load up some data. We will use the iris quality dataset from the UCI website, which is installed along with your R installation. You can check that you have it, by typing in iris at the Command Prompt. You should get 150 rows of data.

If not, then download the data from the UCI website, and rename the file to `iris.csv`. Then, use the **Import Dataset** button on RStudio to import the data.

Now, let's assign the `iris` data to the `data` command. Now, let's look at the data to see if it is loaded correctly. It's enough to look at the first few rows of data, and we will do this by using the `head` command:

```
head(data)
```

Let's look and see how many rows and columns we have for the wine dataset. This will help later, when we look at how many rows we want in the training and the test set:

```
dim(data)
```

When we run this command, we see that we have 150 rows and 5 columns. Let's plot the wine in RStudio so we can see how it looks:

```
plot(data)
```

When we run this command, we get a lattice plot that compares all the variables together. Here is an example:

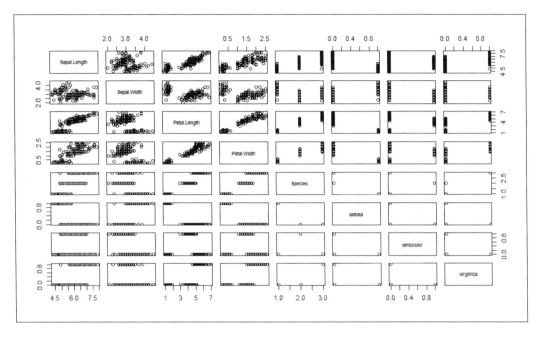

This visualization is quite difficult to read. Let's move forward with the issue of adding more contexts to the data. The following code creates a new column for each of the iris types, and populates the corresponding column with TRUE if the `iris` is of the given type. So, for example, if the `iris` type is `setosa`, then the code returns TRUE in the `setosa` column:

```
data$setosa <- c(data$Species == 'setosa')

data$versicolor <- c(data$Species == 'versicolor')

data$virginica <- c(data$Species == 'virginica')
```

Once we have run these commands, we can use the head command again to see the values. Here is an example result:

```
> head(data)
  Sepal.Length Sepal.Width Petal.Length Petal.Width Species setosa versicolor virginica
1          5.1         3.5          1.4         0.2  setosa   TRUE      FALSE     FALSE
2          4.9         3.0          1.4         0.2  setosa   TRUE      FALSE     FALSE
3          4.7         3.2          1.3         0.2  setosa   TRUE      FALSE     FALSE
4          4.6         3.1          1.5         0.2  setosa   TRUE      FALSE     FALSE
5          5.0         3.6          1.4         0.2  setosa   TRUE      FALSE     FALSE
6          5.4         3.9          1.7         0.4  setosa   TRUE      FALSE     FALSE
```

We could normalize the data before we use it for the neural net. In theory, we don't always need to standardize the inputs to the neural net. The reason for this is that any rescaling of an input could be undone, or redone by any amendment of the corresponding weights and biases. In practice, however, standardizing inputs can make R faster. Therefore, normalizing is one technique that you could consider, particularly when we are handling a lot of data.

Let's start producing Train and Test datasets. We can use the following formula to count the number of rows. Then, we can create an index, which will be used to assign data to either the test or training sets.

Now, we will train the data using set.seed, which allows us to reproduce a particular sequence of random numbers. The seed itself carries no inherent meaning; it's simply a way of telling the random number generator where to start. Here, we are going to set the seed to make the partition reproducible:

```
set.seed(123)
```

Next, we will work out the training and test set. Firstly, we calculate the total number of rows and then we sample the data so that 75 percent of the data is training, and the remainder is test data:

```
totalrows <- nrow(data)
totalrows
samplesize <- floor(0.75 * nrow(data))
```

The samples are indexed separately, using the marker iris_ind. Data with the marker iris_ind goes to the training dataset, and rest of the data goes to the test dataset.

Next, we can assign the data to the training set or the test set:

```
train <- winequality[wine_ind, ]
test <- winequality[-wine_ind, ]
```

Now, we will call the neuralnet function to create a neural network. We are training the data, so we are going to use the training set of data. As a starting point, we are going to work with three hidden layers. The neural network is going to be assigned to the variable nn:

```
nn <- neuralnet(train$setosa + train$versicolor + train$virginica
~ train$Sepal.Length + train$Sepal.Width + train$Petal.Length +
train$Petal.Width, data, hidden=3, lifesign='full')
```

Now we've created the model, let's try to use it with the test data. To do this, we use the predict command, specifying the first four columns:

```
predict <- compute(nn, test[1:4])
```

Now, let's test use this model to predict our results with the test data. In the neuralnet package, this method is used to predict objects of class nn, typically produced by neuralnet.

Firstly, the dataframe is changed by a mean response value, and the data error is worked out between the original response and the new mean response. Then, all duplicate rows are removed to clarify the data.

Eventually, we get our predictions, and we can start to visualize the predicted results of the neural network using Tableau.

Modeling and evaluating data in Tableau

Neural networks are often difficult to understand. When the data is loaded into Tableau, we can visually understand the distinctions made by the underlying model. Since we can easily load data into Tableau, we can do this on an ongoing basis.

In this example, we will use Tableau as part of the testing process. We will present the model with data, and see how well the R model can distinguish between the three types of iris. Once we have set up the Tableau workbook, we can load more data into the workbook, using the connect to data facility. This would help us to see if the model continues to distinguish between the model types, and we could continue to test the model on an ongoing basis.

Using Tableau to evaluate data

Let's load more data into Tableau. For our testing purposes, we will reuse the iris data that we used in the earlier example. However, if this was real life, this would not be the best practice for testing purposes. Here, we are reusing the data so we can be certain that our results in Tableau match our results in R. Then, in real life, we would move forward by using new test data.

To load in the iris dataset, refer to the UCI Machine Learning website. Here is the URL for reference: http://mlr.cs.umass.edu/ml/datasets.html.

Once the data is downloaded and imported into Tableau, you will see the headers appear. Here is an example:

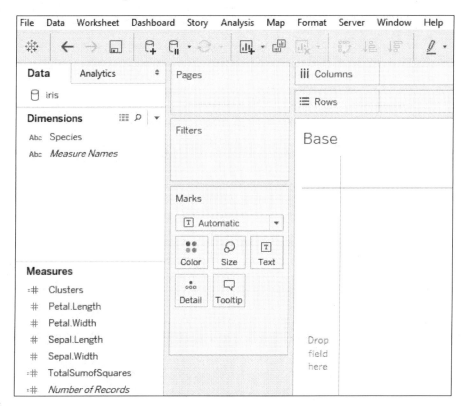

After the data is imported, let's write a small script that will access the neural network in R. Here is the code:

```
SCRIPT_REAL(
'library(neuralnet); predict <- compute(nn,data.frame(.arg1,.arg2,.arg3,.
arg4));predict$net.result[1,]',
SUM([Petal.Length]), SUM([Petal.Width]),SUM([Sepal.Length]),SUM([Sepal.
Width]))
```

Let's break the script down.

Initially, the code calls the `neuralnet` library, so that the rest of the script will run. The predict variable is used to hold the results of the compute format. It needs four arguments to run, and those are the columns in the Tableau notation at the end.

To put the script into Tableau, go to the **Measures** option and right-click to get the menu for **Calculated Fields**. We will put the script into a **Calculated Field**. In our example, we will give it a name: Predicted Output. When we put it into Tableau, it appears as follows:

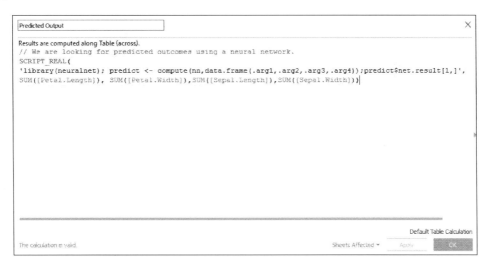

Once the formula is in place, we can look at producing visualizations to show the differences in the cluster. Here, we will start with the end result, and then step back so we can see how it was done:

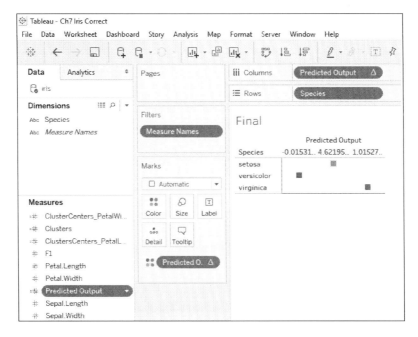

In this example, we can see that the predicted output for each `iris` type is clear, and it's distinct in terms of the actual number, and the actual color.

To create this workbook, we have simply dragged over the `Species` and the `Predicted Output` pills onto the canvas, and used `Predicted Output` for the color. It's great to have visualizations empowered with R, which we can use easily in Tableau.

Summary

In this chapter you have learned how to manipulate data using unsupervised learning techniques and algorithms applying R and Tableau. The usage Tableau is simple; we use it to visualize the analytics. Also we can develop data analytics using it and delivering the overall data science project, by helping business users to evaluate and understand the models that they have been given. We can get the data, analyze it, and evaluate it with a real approach.

In the next chapter we will see how to interpret the results and the numbers, when you have them, how to make them understandable for real applications in real life, applying the data in real situations and visualization.

8
Interpreting Your Results for Your Audience

If we feel a cold, then we use a jacket. When we are hungry, we decide to eat. These decisions can be made by us, but how does a machine make a decision? In this chapter, we will learn how to build a decision system that can be implemented on IoT devices. All of these systems can analyze with all the chapters seen in this book. The main idea of this chapter is to use the analytics algorithms, and to learn how to apply them in IoT projects

We will explore the following topics:

- Introduction to decision system and machine learning
- Building a simple decision system-based Bayesian theory
- Integrating a decision system and IoT project
- Building your own decision system-based IoT

Introduction to decision system and machine learning

A decision system that makes a decision based on several input parameters. A decision system is built on decision theories. Being human involves making decisions for almost all life cases.

The following are examples of decisions that humans make:

- Shall I buy the car today? The decision depends on my preferences. This car looks fine, but it is too expensive for me.

- Shall I bring an umbrella today? This decision depends on the current condition in the area where we are staying. If it is cloudy, it's better to bring an umbrella even though it may not rain.

Generally speaking, we teach a machine such as a computer in order to understand and achieve a specific goal. This case is called machine learning. Varieties of programs are implemented in machines so they can make decisions. Machine learning consists of using various algorithms to build a decision system. In this book, I use fuzzy logic and Bayesian algorithms to make a decision system. I will explain them in the next section.

Decision system-based Bayesian

Bayesian uses the manipulation of conditional probabilities approach to interpret data. In this section, we build a decision system using the Bayesian method. Consider D, called the decision space, which denotes the space of all possible decisions d that could be chosen by the **decision maker** (DM). Θ is the space of all possible outcomes or state of nature ω, $\omega \in \Theta$.

Decision system-based Bayesian is built by Bayesian theory. For illustration, I show a simple spam filter using Bayesian. Imagine the sample space X is the set of all possible datasets of words, from which a single dataset word x will result. For each $\omega \in \Theta$ and $x \in X$, the sampling model $P(\omega)$ describes a belief that x would be the outcome of spam probability. $P(x \mid \omega)$, prior to distribution, is the true population characteristics and supposes a spam probability for x. $P(\omega \mid x)$, posterior distribution, describes a belief that ω is the true value of spam, having observed dataset x.

The posterior distribution is obtained using Bayes' rule as follows:

$$P(\omega \mid x) = \frac{P(x \mid \omega) P(\omega)}{P(x)}$$

This result will return a spam probability value.

Now we can build a decision system. Consider λ (ω,d) as a lost function that states exactly how costly each action d is. Lost function $\lambda(di \,|\, \omega i)$ is the loss incurred for taking action di, where the class is ωi. The expected loss or conditional risk is defined as follows:

$$R\left(d_i \,|\, x\right) = \sum_{j=1}^{c} \lambda\left(d_i \,|\, \omega_j\right) P\left(\omega_j \,|\, x\right)$$

A decision function $d(x)$ is a mapping from observations to actions. The total risk of a decision function can be calculated as given in the following equation:

$$E_{P(x)}\left[R\left(d\left(x\right) \,|\, x\right)\right] = \sum_{x} P\left(x\right) R\left(d\left(x\right) \,|\, x\right)$$

A decision function is optimal if it minimizes the total risk. A decision is made based on a minimum risk value for each action. This is a simple explanation. To get further information about Bayesian theory, I suggest you read a textbook about Bayesian.

Decision system-based fuzzy logic

Consider you want to make a decision based on the current temperature, for instance, if the room's temperature is 30°C, then you turn on a cooler machine. Otherwise, if the room's temperature is 18°C, you turn on a heater machine.

This decision happens because we already defined exact values for turning on the machines. What's happening is that we say that we want to turn on the cooler machine if the room's temperature is hot. Furthermore, we also want to turn on the heater machine if the room's temperature is cold.

Cold and hot are two terms related to human linguistics. We should determine how what cold and hot criteria are. A human differentiates the criteria for cold and hot, but how can a computer and machine know?

This problem can be solved using fuzzy logic. The idea of fuzzy logic was first introduced by *Dr. Lotfi Zadeh* from the University of California at Berkeley in the 1960s. The theory of fuzzy logic is developed with fuzzy sets and memberships.

In general, decision system-based fuzzy logic is described in the following figure:

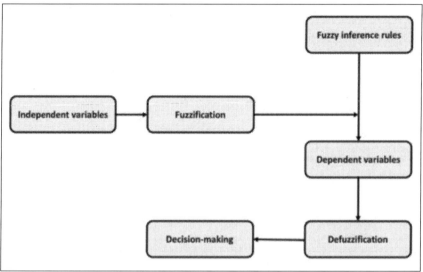

We can build a decision system with the following steps:

- Define independent variables that represent your problem. This step is a part of the extraction process. These variables usually have numeric values.
- Build fuzzy sets that consist of linguistic variables, for instance, cold, warm, and hot.
- Execute the fuzzification process, which transforms independent variables (numerical values) to dependent variables (linguistic values).
- Build fuzzy inference rules to map between a given input and an output. We can use the `if-then` approach.
- After aggregating all outputs, we do defuzzification to obtain a single number.

From the output of a single number, we can make a decision. We will do an experiment on how to build a decision system using fuzzy logic in the next section.

Bayesian Theory

We can implement Bayesian probability using Python. For our demo, we generate output values from two independent variables, x1 and x2. The output model is defined as follows:

$$y = \alpha + \beta_1 x_1 + \beta_2 x_2 + c\sigma$$

c is a random value. We define a, $\beta 1$, $\beta 2$, and σ as 0.5, 1, 2.5, and 0.5.

These independent variables are generated using a random object from the NumPy library. After that, we compute the model with these variables.

We can implement this case with the following scripts:

```
import matplotlib
matplotlib.use('Agg')
import numpy as np
import matplotlib.pyplot as plt
# initialization
np.random.seed(100)
alpha, sigma = 0.5, 0.5
beta = [1, 2.5]
size = 100


# Predictor variable
X1 = np.random.randn(size)
X2 = np.random.randn(size) * 0.37
# Simulate outcome variable
Y = alpha + beta[0]*X1 + beta[1]*X2 + np.random.randn(size)*sigma
fig, ax = plt.subplots(1, 2, sharex=True, figsize=(10, 4))
fig.subplots_adjust(bottom=0.15, left=0.1)
ax[0].scatter(X1, Y)
ax[1].scatter(X2, Y)
ax[0].set_ylabel('Y')
ax[0].set_xlabel('X1')
ax[1].set_xlabel('X2')
plt.grid(True)
fig.savefig('predict.png', dpi=100)
print("finish")
```

You can save these scripts into a file, called `ch02_predict.py`.

Here is the result of getting the data:

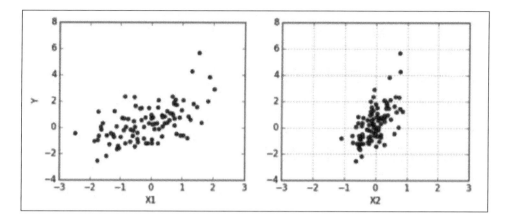

This program will also generate three files, `alpha.png`, `beta.png`, and `theta-3.png`. A sample of the alpha.png file is depicted in the following figure:

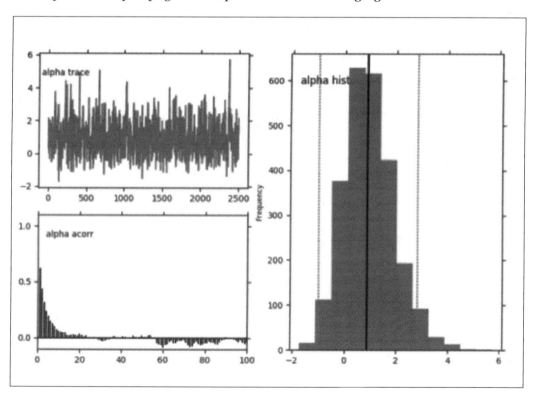

You can see alpha values, which are random values with normal distribution `alpha.png`. Furthermore, beta values are generated with normal distribution. You can see beta values in the `beta.png` file in the following figure:

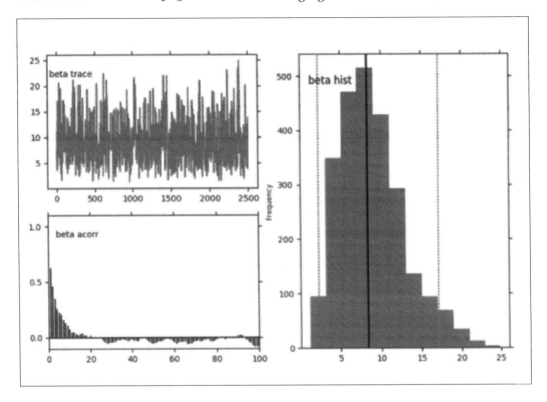

The last of the program output is the theta-3.png file, which shows how theta values are computed by a formula. You can see it in the following figure:

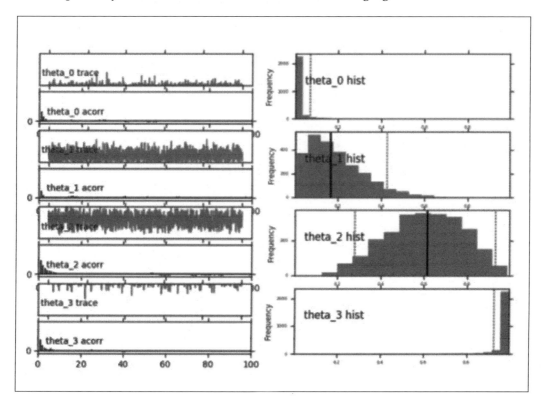

Fuzzy logic

One of the famous Python libraries for fuzzy logic is `scikit-fuzzy`. Several fuzzy logic algorithms have already been implemented on this library. Since `scikit-fuzzy` is an open source library, you can review the source code at https:// github.com/ scikit-fuzzy/scikit-fuzzy.

Before you install this library, you should already have installed `NumPy` and `SciPy` libraries. You can install `scikit-fuzzy` using `pip`, by typing the following command:

```
$ sudo pip install scikit-fuzzy
```

As another option, you can install the `scikit-fuzzy` library from source code.

Type these commands:

```
$ git clone https://github.com/scikit-fuzzy/scikit-fuzzy
$ cd scikit-fuzzy/
$ sudo python setup.py install
```

After completing the installation, you can use scikit-fuzzy. To test how to work with scikit-fuzzy, we will build a fuzzy membership for temperature using the fuzz.trimf() function. You can write the following scripts:

```python
import matplotlib
matplotlib.use('Agg')

import numpy as np
import skfuzzy as fuzz
import matplotlib.pyplot as plt

# Generate universe variables
x_temp = np.arange(0, 11, 1)

# Generate fuzzy membership functions
temp_lo = fuzz.trimf(x_temp, [0, 0, 5])
temp_md = fuzz.trimf(x_temp, [0, 5, 10])
temp_hi = fuzz.trimf(x_temp, [5, 10, 10])

# Visualize these universes and membership functions
fig, ax = plt.subplots()
ax.plot(x_temp, temp_lo, 'b--', linewidth=1.5, label='Cold')
ax.plot(x_temp, temp_md, 'g-', linewidth=1.5, label='Warm')
ax.plot(x_temp, temp_hi, 'r:', linewidth=1.5, label='Hot')
ax.set_title('Temperature')
ax.legend()
ax.spines['top'].set_visible(False)
ax.spines['right'].set_visible(False)
ax.get_xaxis().tick_bottom()
ax.get_yaxis().tick_left()
```

```
ax.set_ylabel('Fuzzy membership')


plt.tight_layout()
print('saving...')
plt.grid(True)
fig.savefig('fuzzy_membership.png', dpi=100)
print('done')
```

This program will generate a `fuzzy_membership.png` file. A sample of this file is depicted as follows:

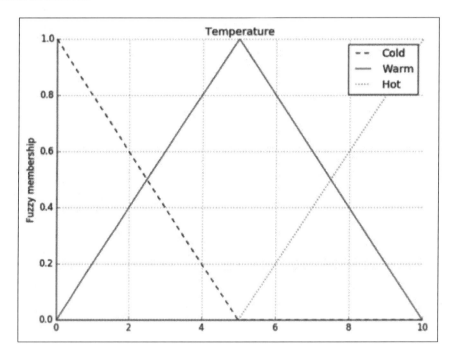

Building a simple decision system-based Bayesian theory

In this section, we build a simple decision system using Bayesian theory. A smart water system is a smart system that controls water. In general, you can see the system architecture in the following figure:

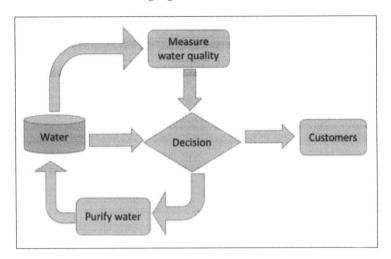

After using a sensing process on water to obtain the water quality, you can make a decision. If the water quality is good, we can transfer the water to customers. Otherwise, we purify the water.

To implement a decision system-based Bayesian theory, firstly we define the state of nature. In this case, we define two states of nature:

- $\omega 1$: Water is ready for drinking
- $\omega 2$: Water should be cleaned (kotor)

For inputs, we can declare x_1 and x_2 as negative and positive as the observation results. We define prior values and class conditional probabilities as follows:

$$P(\omega_1) = 0.8$$
$$P(\omega_2) = 0.2$$
$$P(x_1 \mid \omega_1) = 0.3$$
$$P(x_1 \mid \omega_2) = 0.7$$
$$P(x_2 \mid \omega_1) = 0.2$$
$$P(x_2 \mid \omega_2) = 0.8$$

To build a decision, we should make a loss function. The following is a loss function for our program:

$$\lambda(d_1 \mid \omega_1) = 0$$
$$\lambda(d_1 \mid \omega_2) = 5$$
$$\lambda(d_2 \mid \omega_1) = 10$$
$$\lambda(d_2 \mid \omega_2) = 0$$

Integrating a decision system and IoT project

IoT boards help us to perform sensing and actuating. To build a decision system with IoT boards, we can use a sensing process on IoT boards as input parameters for our decision system. After performing decision computing, we can make some actions through actuating on IoT boards.

In general, we can integrate our decision system with IoT boards, as shown in the following figure:

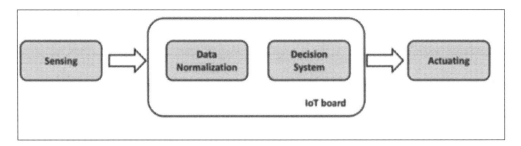

Several sensor devices can be attached to the IoT board that is used for sensing. Depending on what you need; you can gather environmental data, such as temperature, as digital inputs that will be used for our decision system. You can see samples of sensor devices in the following figure:

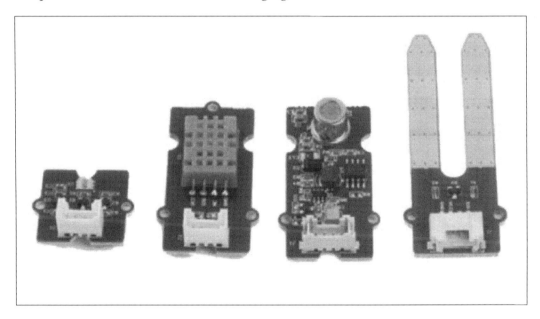

Several actuator devices can be used in our decision system. Each final output from a system can be mapped into an action. This action can be represented as turning on an actuator device.

Some systems may not do sensing on their environment to gather input data. We can obtain data from a database or another system through a network.

Building your own decision system-based IoT

In this section, we build a simple decision system using fuzzy logic on Raspberry Pi. We use Python for implementation. We build a system to monitor temperature and humidity in a room to decide if the environment is comfortable or not. If the environment is not comfortable, then we turn on a cooler machine.

The following is our design system:

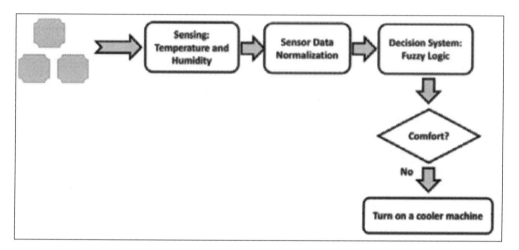

Wiring

We use **DHT22** and relay modules for our wiring. Connect the **DHT22** module into the following connections:

- DHT22 pin 1 (VDD) is connected to the 3.3V pin from Raspberry Pi
- DHT22 pin 2 (SIG) is connected to the GPIO23 (see the BCM column) pin from Raspberry Pi
- DHT22 pin 4 (GND) is connected to the GND pin from Raspberry Pi
- A relay VCC is connected to the 3.3V pin from Raspberry Pi
- A relay GND is connected to the GND pin from Raspberry Pi
- A relay signal is connected to the GPIO26 (see the BCM column) pin from Raspberry Pi

The complete wiring is shown in the following figure:

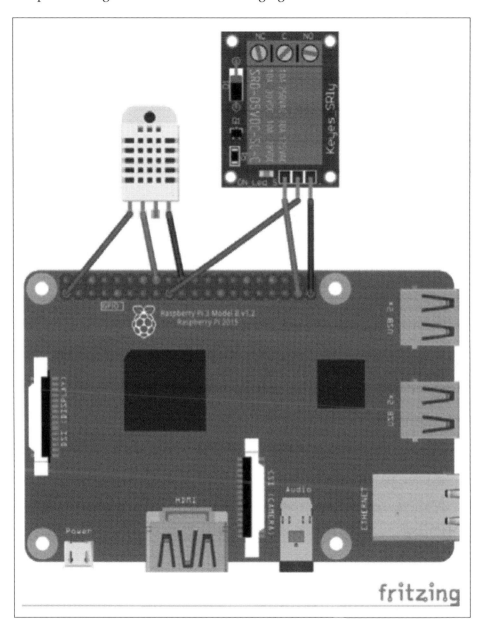

Writing the program

We build a fuzzy logic to implement a decision system. Two inputs from the sensing are temperature and humidity. In this case, we start developing a fuzzy membership for temperature and humidity. For testing, I build the following fuzzy membership models for temperature and humidity, which are shown in the following figure:

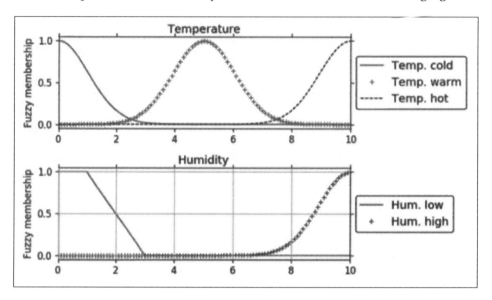

In the temperature model, we create three categories: cold, warm, and hot. Also, we make two categories for humidity: low and high.

The code:

```
import matplotlib
matplotlib.use('Agg')
import numpy as np
import skfuzzy as fuzz
import matplotlib.pyplot as plt
import Adafruit_DHT
import RPi.GPIO as GPIO
import time
```

After that, we initialize Raspberry Pi GPIO for DHT22 and the relay module:

```
print('initialization...')


### initialization GPIO
relay_pin = 26
GPIO.setmode(GPIO.BCM)
GPIO.setup(relay_pin, GPIO.OUT)
sensor = Adafruit_DHT.DHT22
# DHT22 pin on Raspberry Pi
dht_pin = 23
```

The next step is to build a fuzzy logic model by starting to create fuzzy membership for temperature and humidity.

We create the `temperature_category()` and `humidity_category()` functions to map from sensing input to system:

```
########## INPUTS #######################
#Input Universe functions
temperature = np.arange(0, 11, 0.1)
humidity = np.arange(0, 11, 0.1)


# Input Membership Functions
# Temperature
temperature_cold = fuzz.gaussmf(temperature, 0, 1.5)
temperature_warm = fuzz.gaussmf(temperature, 5, 1.5)
temperature_hot = fuzz.gaussmf(temperature, 10, 1.5)


# Humidity
humidity_low = fuzz.trapmf(humidity, [0, 0, 1, 3])
humidity_high = fuzz.gaussmf(humidity, 10, 1.5)



########## OUTPUT #######################
# comfort
```

```
# Output Variables Domain
comfort = np.arange(0, 30, 0.1)


# Output Membership Function


comfort_low = fuzz.trimf(comfort, [0, 5, 10])
comfort_ave = fuzz.trimf(comfort, [10, 15, 25])
comfort_very = fuzz.trimf(comfort, [20, 25, 30])
def temperature_category(temperature_in=18):



temperature_cat_cold = fuzz.interp_membership(temperature,
temperature_cold, temperature_in)
temperature_cat_warm = fuzz.interp_membership(temperature,
temperature_warm, temperature_in)
temperature_cat_hot = fuzz.interp_membership(temperature,
temperature_hot, temperature_in)
return dict(cold=temperature_cat_cold, warm=temperature_cat_warm,
hot=temperature_cat_hot)


def humidity_category(humidity_in=2):
humidity_cat_low = fuzz.interp_membership(humidity, humidity_low,
humidity_in)
humidity_cat_high = fuzz.interp_membership(humidity, humidity_
high, humidity_in)
return dict(low=humidity_cat_low, high=humidity_cat_high)
```

We also print our membership for reference into a file. It's done using a `matplotlib` library. We save fuzzy memberships for temperature and humidity:

```
# print membership
# Visualize these universes and membership functions


print('saving membership...')
fig, ax = plt.subplots(2, 1)
[t1, t2, t3] = ax[0].plot(temperature, temperature_cold, 'r',
temperature, temperature_warm, 'm+', temperature,
```

```
temperature_hot, 'b--', label=['Temp. cold',
'Temp. warm', 'Temp. hot'])


ax[0].set_ylabel('Fuzzy membership')
ax[0].set_title('Temperature')
ax[0].set_ylim(-0.05, 1.05)
ax[0].set_xlim(0, 10)



lgd1 = ax[0].legend([t1, t2, t3], ['Temp. cold', 'Temp. warm', 'Temp.
hot'], loc='center left', bbox_to_anchor=(1, 0.5))

[t1, t2] = ax[1].plot(humidity, humidity_low, 'r', humidity, humidity_
high, 'b+')
ax[1].set_ylabel('Fuzzy membership')
ax[1].set_title('Humidity')
ax[1].set_ylim(-0.05, 1.05)
ax[1].set_xlim(0, 10)



lgd2 = ax[1].legend([t1, t2], ['Hum. low', 'Hum. high'], loc='center
left', bbox_to_anchor=(1, 0.5))

plt.grid(True)
plt.tight_layout()
plt.show()

fig.savefig('fuzzy_mem_temp_hum.png', dpi=100, bbox_extra_
artists=(lgd1, lgd2, ), bbox_inches='tight')
print('done')
```

Now we are ready to read temperature and humidity via the DHT22 module. Then, we compute them into our fuzzy logic system. Furthermore, we make fuzzy inferences from our input data. We do fuzzy aggregation to generate the output.

The output is a numeric form. We can map it as low, average, and very comfortable. From this situation, we can make a decision about whether we want to turn a cooler machine on or not:

```python
# sensing and make decision
print('program is ready for making decision based fuzzy logic')
machine_state = -1
try:
    while 1:
        print('sensing...')
        sen_humidity, sen_temperature = Adafruit_DHT.read_retry(sensor,
dht_pin)

        if humidity is not None and temperature is not None:
            print('Sensing: Temperature={0:0.1f}*C  Humidity={1:0.1f}%'.
format(sen_temperature, sen_humidity))

            sen_temperature = 18
            sen_humidity = 80
            # normalization
            norm_temperature = sen_temperature / 60.0
            norm_humidity = sen_humidity / 100.0
            print('Normalization: Temperature={0:0.0001f}
Humidity={1:0.0001f}'
                .format(norm_temperature, norm_humidity))

            temp_in = temperature_category(norm_temperature)
            hum_in = humidity_category(norm_humidity)
            print('fuzzy membership: Temperature={0}  Humidity={1}'.
format(temp_in, hum_in))

            # Determine the weight and aggregate
            rule1 = np.fmax(temp_in['hot'], hum_in['low'])
            rule2 = temp_in['warm']
            rule3 = np.fmax(temp_in['warm'], hum_in['high'])

            imp1 = np.fmin(rule1, comfort_low)
```

```
            imp2 = np.fmin(rule2, comfort_ave)
            imp3 = np.fmin(rule3, comfort_very)


            aggregate_membership = np.fmax(imp1, imp2, imp3)


            # Defuzzify
            result_comfort = fuzz.defuzz(comfort, aggregate_membership,
'centroid')
            print(result_comfort)


            # make decision based on experiment
            if result_comfort >= 5.002:
                if machine_state < 0:
                    machine_state = 1
                    print("turn on a machine")
                    GPIO.output(relay_pin, GPIO.HIGH)
                else:
                    print("a machine already turn on")
            else:
                if machine_state > 0:
                    machine_state = 0
                    print("turn off a machine")
                    GPIO.output(relay_pin, GPIO.LOW)
                else:
                    print("a machine already turn off")


            time.sleep(2)


        time.sleep(2)


except KeyboardInterrupt:
    GPIO.output(relay_pin, GPIO.LOW)
    GPIO.cleanup()
```

Testing

In the following screenshot we can see the results of measurements of the system acquiring data from sensors:

```
● ● ●      Documents — pi@raspberrypi: ~/Documents/book — ssh pi@192.168.0.12 — 8...
[pi@raspberrypi:~/Documents/book $ sudo python ch02_fuzzy.py
initialization...
saving membership...
done
program is ready for making decision based fuzzy logic
sensing...
Sensing: Temperature=28.6*C  Humidity=85.0%
Normalization: Temperature=0.3  Humidity=0.8
fuzzy membership: Temperature={'hot': 6.8987413995925987e-19, 'warm': 5.44745042
4466365e-05, 'cold': 0.96078943915232318}  Humidity={'high': 4.6005175273896544e
-17, 'low': 1.0}
5.00202884593
turn on a machine
sensing...
Sensing: Temperature=28.6*C  Humidity=85.1%
Normalization: Temperature=0.3  Humidity=0.8
fuzzy membership: Temperature={'hot': 6.8987413995925987e-19, 'warm': 5.44745042
4466365e-05, 'cold': 0.96078943915232318}  Humidity={'high': 4.6005175273896544e
-17, 'low': 1.0}
5.00202884593
a machine already turn on
sensing...
Sensing: Temperature=28.6*C  Humidity=85.0%
Normalization: Temperature=0.3  Humidity=0.8
fuzzy membership: Temperature={'hot': 6.8987413995925987e-19, 'warm': 5.44745042
4466365e-05, 'cold': 0.96078943915232318}  Humidity={'high': 4.6005175273896544e
-17, 'low': 1.0}
5.00202884593
a machine already turn on
sensing...
Sensing: Temperature=28.6*C  Humidity=85.1%
Normalization: Temperature=0.3  Humidity=0.8
fuzzy membership: Temperature={'hot': 6.8987413995925987e-19, 'warm': 5.44745042
```

Enhancement

This program is a sample of how to use fuzzy logic to develop a decision system. There are many ways you can improve this program. The following is an improvement area to which you can contribute:

- Modify the fuzzy membership model to improve the definition of comfort
- Add more input data to improve accuracy
- Add fuzzy inference methods to obtain the aggregation value

Summary

We have reviewed some basic decision systems by taking two samples, that is, Bayesian and fuzzy logic. We also explored Python libraries for implementing Bayesian and fuzzy logic and then practiced with them. As the last topic, we deployed a decision system using fuzzy logic as a study sample on how to integrate a decision system on an IoT project with Raspberry Pi.

References

The following is a list of recommended books where you can learn more about the topics in this chapter:

- *Introduction to Machine Learning*, *Ethem Alpaydin*, The MIT Press, 2004.

- *A First Course in Bayesian Statistical Methods*, *Peter D. Hoff*. Springer, New York, 2009.

- *Bayes' Rule*: *A Tutorial Introduction to Bayesian Analysis*, *James V Stone*. Sebte Press. 2013.

- *Bayesian risk management*: *A guide to model risk and sequential learning in financial markets*, *Matt Sekerke*. Wiley & Sons. 2015.

- *Fuzzy logic with engineering applications*, 3rd Edition, *Timothy J. Ross*, John Wiley & Sons. 2010.

- *A First Course in Fuzzy Logic*, 3rd Edition, *Hung T. Nguyen* and *Elbert A. Walker*, CRC Press. 2006.

Index

K

k-means clustering
  about 102
  working 103

L

leverage
  versus residuals 60
Lift curves 119
lift scores 121
lists 16
Lloyd algorithm 109
lm()
  used, for conducting simple linear
      regression 52-56
logical operators 27
low p-value 71

M

machine learning 130
matrices 17
Maximum Likelihood Estimate (MLE) 92
model deployment 88, 89
modeling
  in R 85-87
Model Sum of Squares 112
multiple regression 66
multiple regression model
  building 66, 67

N

named list 16
neural network, in R 122-125
neural network model
  evaluating 118
neural network performance measures
  lift scores 121
  Precision and Recall curve 120
  Receiver Operating Characteristic
      curve 119, 120
neural network results
  visualizing 121

neural networks
  about 115
  layers 115
  structure 117
  types 116
normal Q-Q 60

O

Ordinary Least Squares (OLS) 53

P

Pearson's correlation coefficient 59
Pearson's R 59
perceptron 116
populated data frame
  example 18
Precision/Recall curves 119
predicted results
  actual values, comparing with 58
predictor 72
p-value 71, 112

R

R
  decision trees, in Tableau 90
  installing, for Windows 2-7
Random Forest classifier 90
Receiver Operator Characteristic (ROC) 119
Receiver Operator Characteristic (ROC)
      curve 119
regression
  about 51
  business question, solving 70
  multiple regression 66
  simple linear regression 52
relationships
  investigating, in data 59
Relevant Analysis of variance statistics,
      Tableau clustering
  degrees of freedom 112
  Error Sum of Squares 113
  F-statistic 112
  Model Sum of Squares 112
  p-value 112

residuals
about 70
versus fitted 60
versus leverage 60
residual standard error 58
R, from CRAN website
download link 2
RGui 7
R language 113
Root Mean Square Deviation 71
Root Mean Square Error 71
R programming
control structures 27
core essentials 15
data structures 16
Rserve
installing 12, 13
R connectivity 11
Tableau connectivity 11
Rserve connection
configuring 13
RStudio
about 8
download link 8
installation prerequisites 8-10
R website
reference 2
R, with Tableau
results, replicating 61-65

S

scale location 61
scaling 109
scikit-fuzzy
about 136
reference 136
scripting
testing 11
scripts
implementing 10, 11
simple decision system-based Bayesian theory
building 139
simple linear regression
about 52
conducting, lm() used 52-56

StackOverflow
reference 27
statistics
about 74
for clustering 110
supervised learning 67

T

Tableau
data, evaluating 125-128
data, modeling 125
R, improving 31
used, for sharing data analysis 74
Tableau group
creating, from cluster results 106
Tapply 29
Team Data Science Process
about 37
business understanding 38
data acquisition 38
data understanding 38
deployment phase 38
modeling phase 38
summary 39
training material, GitHub
reference 10

U

undirected graphs 96

V

variables
about 15
creating 15, 16
working with 16
vector 16
vectorization 28, 30
vertices 96

W

WDI package
reference 40
Windows
R, installing for 2-7
World Development Indicators (WDI) 41